Lovelock and Gaia

Signs of Life

Jon Turney

REVOLUTIONS IN SCIENCE
Published by Icon Books UK

Published in the UK in 2003
by Icon Books Ltd., Grange Road,
Duxford, Cambridge CB2 4QF
E-mail: info@iconbooks.co.uk
www.iconbooks.co.uk

Published in Australia in 2003
by Allen & Unwin Pty. Ltd.,
PO Box 8500,
83 Alexander Street,
Crows Nest, NSW 2065

Sold in the UK, Europe, South Africa
and Asia by Faber and Faber Ltd.,
3 Queen Square, London WC1N 3AU
or their agents

Distributed in Canada by
Penguin Books Canada,
10 Alcorn Avenue, Suite 300,
Toronto, Ontario M4V 3B2

Distributed in the UK, Europe,
South Africa and Asia by
Macmillan Distribution Ltd.,
Houndmills, Basingstoke RG21 6XS

ISBN 1 84046 458 5

Series editor: Jon Turney

Originating editor: Simon Flynn

Typesetting by Hands Fotoset

Printed and bound in the UK by
Mackays of Chatham plc

For Eleanor and Catherine,
my favourite signs of life.

CONTENTS

Contents

LIST OF ILLUSTRATIONS

ACKNOWLEDGEMENTS

Thanks to colleagues in the Department of Science and Technology Studies at University College London for enriching my ideas about scientific controversy over the last ten years, and to those at the *Times Higher Education Supplement*, for whom I first wrote about Gaia and Spaceship Earth some years before that. Extra thanks to Jane Gregory for hard-to-find materials on Gaia, especially from *Co-Evolution Quarterly*. Will van Zwanenberg's undergraduate dissertation was also a bibliographic inspiration. UCL Library, the University of London Library at Senate House and the British Library were essential, as always. I chose not to contact Jim Lovelock while this book was being written, as he has published so extensively. But he kindly read the penultimate proofs, and corrected some factual errors.

I am also grateful to Andrew Watson for allowing me to read his paper on *Gaia and Observer Self-Selection* while still in press, and to Fred Pearce and Simon Flynn for positive feedback. Danielle read the whole thing, and reined in my sarcasm about the 'new age'. Eleanor read some, too, until homework intervened. If Gaia ever gets into the UK's National Curriculum, she may one day have time to read the rest.

· CHAPTER I ·

GOLDILOCKS' PLANET

> [O]*ur own planet earth ... It is the strangest of all*
> *places, and there is everything in the world to learn*
> *about it.*
>
> Lewis Thomas

Take out a match and strike it. Friction heats a mix of chemicals and light flares at the head. Perfected in the nineteenth century, portable fire is a nice everyday testament to human ingenuity.

And to something else. The most remarkable thing about the match is that those chemicals are used up in the first flare. Yet the stick goes on burning. It is just one example – repeated hundreds of millions of times a day – of the fact that much of the stuff of our world lies just a few degrees the right side of ignition. Like every other fire – whether a forest blaze sparked by a discarded cigarette, a brazier on a chilly building site, or just your gas stove – every match relies on the fact that the oxygen in our atmosphere makes it alarmingly reactive.

Nor is oxygen the only reactive gas enveloping the Earth. There's a small amount of methane, for example, which combines eagerly with oxygen, but remains at a roughly constant level. Something seems to be keeping the whole atmosphere poised in this unstable state. It is, a chemist would say, far from equilibrium.

As it happens, the concentration of oxygen is in a range which suits the evolution of large, lumbering collections of cells like human beings. Of course it has to be, or else we would not be here to remark on the fact. But it is still intriguing that the proportion of atmospheric oxygen on Earth – around 21 per cent – is just enough to allow respiration to generate the energy that a large creature needs, but just too low to lead to spontaneous combustion of dry vegetation. And it seems to have stayed that way for aeons.

If some cosmic estate agent sold planets, they could point to lots of other features of the Earth which would make it a comfortable home. Note the extensive oceans, which are salty but not too salty. Feel the temperature, not too hot, not too cold. It is as if Goldilocks stumbled across a cottage in which not just one of each, but all the things she found were 'just right'. And there is a fire burning merrily behind the grate. But why?

For some, the explanation for our atmosphere balancing on an almost-but-not-quite-explosive knife edge is that life likes it that way. More generally, thinking about the atmosphere and other features of our planet suggests a grand hypothesis: that all the living things on Earth somehow act together to influence the whole environment, and that influence helps maintain conditions which suit them. To put it more emphatically, the Earth is alive. Oh, and unlike most scientific hypotheses, this one was named after an ancient deity – Gaia, the Greek goddess of the Earth.

The Gaia hypothesis was first formulated in the 1960s, and met with widespread indifference. It was simply too far out of line with the way most Earth scientists were thinking about their subject to be heard clearly. When it was popularised at book length in the late 1970s the response was much more varied and interesting. The idea of the living Earth was taken up or denounced by a host of groups for a host of reasons. Gaia attracted a few scientific supporters, and many opponents. Outside science, it drew quasi-religious devotion from some environmentalists and from prophets of 'New Age' ideas. And this evoked yet further hostile reactions. One of the scientific supporters, microbiologist Lynn Margulis, and her science-writing son Dorion Sagan suggest that 'a cursory sociological study would reveal that [Gaia] has been attacked not only for being unscientific and "untestable", but as antihuman polemics, green politics, industrial apologetics, and even as non-Christian ecological "satanism"'. As they say, such a range of critics suggests that the power of Gaia goes beyond science. It also indicates that some of the scientific reservations were fuelled by a wariness about Gaia as a religious cult, or a new 'way of knowing', among researchers who had been finding their old ways of knowing pretty productive.

Thirty years later, Gaia is still controversial, but has many more scientific sympathisers. Under the guise of the more neutral-sounding 'geophysiology', or the more formal 'Earth system science', some aspects of Gaian thinking have become almost respectable in polite scientific circles. There are still doubts about the strongest versions of the Gaia hypothesis. But at the very least, it has spawned a real research programme which is yielding new insights into how earth, air, oceans

4

and organisms interact. Could Gaia, at its grandest, turn out to be that rarity, a genuine scientific revolution in the making? We shall see.

This book charts the origins and growth of the Gaia hypothesis, and describes its scientific development. We will meet its major scientific proponents, who include some of the most interesting scientists of the last half-century, and its detractors, some of whom are also important researchers. We will consider alternative explanations for the features of the Earth which Gaia theory tries to account for, and look at the kind of tactics which have been used in the debates about which are most plausible. We will see how opinion has moved and, briefly, review the current state of the evidence for some Gaian effects.

While the story which follows concentrates on the scientific side of the argument, this cannot really be separated from the wider social and cultural currents of the last four decades. The rise of both scientific and popular ecology (the overlap is partial, at best), partly summed up by the slogan that 'everything is connected to everything else', the growing appeal of systems thinking and of ideas like the emergence of higher-level properties in complex assemblies of simpler components, have all played their part in increasing sympathy for Gaia. And from the controversies over fallout from nuclear testing in the 1950s, through the concerns about pollution crystallised by Rachel Carson's *Silent Spring* in 1962, to more recent anxieties over the depletion of atmospheric ozone and global climate change, we have all become more conscious of the effects one particular living species may be having on the whole planet. A little book like this cannot do justice to that history, but we will pause here and there to consider the Gaian view of planetary life in relation to these more immediate concerns.

But scientifically speaking, before looking at whether Gaia theory is the best explanation for the comforts of home, we need to ask how they came to be seen as in need of explanation. One answer lies, not in Earth science, strictly defined, but in the growing interest in other planets born of the space programmes of the second half of the twentieth century. Specifically, it lies on Mars, and in the contemplation of Mars by an unusual Englishman, James Lovelock.

CHAPTER II

ORIGINS

Going to Mars? Don't bother

> *[M]oments of intuition do not come from an empty mind; they require the gathering together of many apparently unconnected facts …*
>
> James Lovelock

According to its originator, the first inklings of what grew into the Gaia hypothesis can be dated pretty precisely. 'The intuition that the Earth controls its surface and atmosphere to keep the environment always benign for life came to me one afternoon in September 1965 at the Jet Propulsion Laboratory (JPL) in California', he writes. James Lovelock was an Englishman abroad, in his mid-40s, and enjoying his fourth year of consulting for the American National Aeronautics and Space Administration. NASA was a young organisation, constituted in 1958 when it inherited the USA's former military space programmes. It had already played a part in turning Earth science into planetary science in its satellites' contributions to the world-wide International Geophysical Year of the late 1950s. A few years later, NASA was in the throes of the Apollo programme which would put men on the Moon in 1969, but in those expansive days it was also thinking about missions to Mars. Lovelock, who had a reputation for inventing ingenious devices to detect small amounts of chemicals, was brought in to help with the most tantalising aspect of those missions. The Moon was obviously dead, but could there be life on Mars? And how would we know?

Never slow to doubt established thinking, the new scientific visitor lost no time in questioning the existing plans for detecting life on a strange planet. These were too specific, he argued, and assumed that any Martian life would show traces of chemicals found in terrestrial organisms. What was needed was something more general. The most general way he could think of was a way of detecting entropy-reduction, where entropy is the physicist's term for the degree of disorder in a system. The most general version of one of the most famous scientific principles, the Second Law of Thermodynamics, says that entropy always tends to increase. Living systems always appear to fight this tendency. Life increases complexity, which means that local entropy decreases. The energy which maintains this complexity ultimately comes from nuclear reactions in stars, which ensures that overall entropy always increases, but it is a neat trick all the same.

Challenged to think of an experiment which would register entropy reduction, Lovelock read the physicist Erwin Schrödinger's famous book of 1944, *What is Life?* This prescient work influenced many of the scientists who worked on the structure of genes and DNA after the Second World War, but also discussed how life achieves its small-scale victories against the Second Law. It does so by evolving tightly coupled to its environment, extracting order, as it were, from a larger system. The new preoccupation with Mars encouraged the thought that the larger system might be planet-sized.

The first glimmerings of Gaia put this together with some basic thoughts about how organisms and environments interact. If a living cell is exchanging chemicals with the outside world, there must be a means of moving the chemicals around, removing wastes and bringing nutrients within reach. The only two ways of doing this, the only media for transport and exchange, are air or water. As it looked like there was no liquid water left on Mars, what passes for air on the planet was the only thing left for life to use.

Hence Lovelock's eventual answer for NASA. The simplest way of showing up a persistent reduction in entropy produced by some kind of life would be to analyse the mixture of gases in the Martian atmosphere. If they were at chemical equilibrium, with no molecules floating around which could reduce their total energy by reacting together, there was little chance that life existed. If, on the other hand, the atmosphere was shifted from equilibrium, this could well be because living organisms were drawing some gases preferentially from the atmosphere, while releasing others.

The politics of this idea, which Lovelock developed with a young NASA official called Dian Hitchcock who was sent to JPL to review the biology experiments, were delicate. It might make sense to send a spacecraft all the way to Mars to scoop soil samples. However, the subtleties of chemical spectroscopy meant that the composition of the atmosphere could be worked out using earthbound telescopes. So NASA's new consultant on Mars missions was effectively telling them not to bother going there. But although modified versions of the original Mars-based experiments went ahead, Lovelock stayed on the team.

Some months later, on his latest visit to JPL, he was able to look in detail at new data on the atmospheres of Mars and Venus captured by a French observatory using an infra-red telescope. These showed clearly that both planets had inert atmospheres dominated by carbon dioxide. Primed by his ideas about life detection, Lovelock was now struck forcibly by how different the Earth's atmosphere looked. With its large amounts of nitrogen and oxygen, a mere trace of carbon dioxide, and appreciable doses of other reactive gases like methane, our planet was in 'exuberant disequilibrium'. And it seemed to him that life must be keeping it that way.

One of the people he tried the idea out on straight away was the astronomer – and future media star – Carl Sagan, deeply interested in planets and in life. Sagan's reaction was muted, but he mentioned that there was another puzzle about the Earth. It appeared to have maintained stable temperatures even though standard stellar models had long indicated that the Sun has gradually grown hotter and hotter, perhaps by as much as 30 per cent since the planet formed billions of years ago. Neither of these features of the deep past of the Earth was completely certain, then or now, but there seemed to be good evidence for both. Immediately, Lovelock was tempted to incorporate climate into his embryonic scheme for planetary regulation. In fact, he glimpsed a larger, more general idea: 'Suddenly the image of the Earth as a living organism able to regulate its temperature and chemistry at a comfortable steady state emerged in my mind.' Here was the beginning of Gaia, although the hypothesis was yet to be named. But why did the idea occur to this particular Englishman?

An independent scientist

[A] *sensitive man with a deep sense of intellectual mischief …*

Dorion Sagan and Lynn Margulis

His dalliance with the US space programme, and hence with one of the largest science and technology bureaucracies ever created, was one of the things which made it possible for James Lovelock to formulate the Gaia hypothesis. Others were more personal.

He was born in 1919 and brought up in Brixton in South London, though with long spells in the country which affected his outlook deeply. He spent his youth captivated by science and repelled by formal schooling. Fortunately, the precociously self-sufficient boy learnt enough from library books and his own experiments to get a school-leaver's job as a laboratory assistant in a firm of consultant chemists. This small company was run by an ex-academic from London's Imperial College who had decided to go independent. But unlike his young protégé's later career, he did so not to pursue his own research but on strictly commercial terms, mainly serving the photographic trade. Through the day-to-day problem-solving of a company that did whatever customers wanted, Lovelock had an unbeatable hands-on introduction to applied chemistry, and enrolled as an evening student at Birkbeck College, also in London, to formalise his knowledge. The outbreak of war then took him to Manchester to complete his studies as a full-time student. On arriving there, he proved so skilled at chemical analysis that the professor accused him of making up his results, until he saw him do the work in person.

The young Lovelock was a left-winger and, under

Quaker influence, a pacifist, and registered as a conscientious objector despite a student's exemption from military service. After graduation in 1941, a job at the National Institute for Medical Research answered the imperatives of science and conscience, and he began a twenty-year stint there during which he worked on a startling range of projects. The Institute was then run in a style which few scientists today would recognise. It was funded by the state through the Medical Research Council, the oldest of Britain's research councils, class-ridden but largely free of bureaucratic fetters. Scientific staff were expected to follow their own ideas, a habit which reinforced Lovelock's later distaste for what he saw as the conservatism of the 'peer review' system for awarding grants. In this free and easy intellectual atmosphere he worked on 'air hygiene' – airborne transport of bacteria – virology, the common cold, calcium in blood clotting, monitoring cattle movements, and protecting cells (and eventually whole animals) from damage through freezing. All the while, he was a chemist among biologists, but also a resourceful fixer who delighted in developing ingenious solutions to others' technical problems. In his last years at the Institute, in its post-war headquarters at Mill Hill in

North London, he moved to the biochemistry division to work on chemical detectors.

This work centred on the new technique of gas chromatography. Liquid chromatography had long been indispensable as a method for separating complex mixtures. It worked by dribbling a solution down a tall column of some inert substance. The physical properties of the various molecules – their size and electrical charges – meant that they passed down the column at different rates, and could be washed out of the bottom one at a time. The technique was called chromatography as it was first used to separate coloured pigments from flowers. In the early 1950s, the same idea was being applied to gas and vapour mixtures. This could separate extremely small quantities of unknown substances, but how to register their presence when they came off the column?

Lovelock's combination of practical skills with chemical and physical intuition was perfect for this problem, and he poured out a stream of inventions for ever more sensitive detectors. The most important of these, by common consent, was the so-called Electron Capture Detector (ECD). This little device was vital for his future career, as well as playing a crucial role in the environmental politics

15

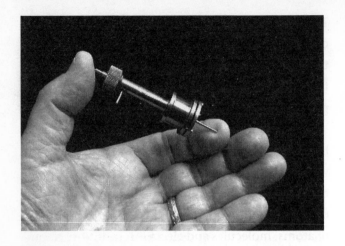

Figure 1. Electron Capture Detector. Lovelock's electron capture detector is a small and exquisitely sensitive instrument for sniffing out trace chemicals.

of the coming decades. Here's how it works. A small radioactive source is installed inside a tube of nitrogen gas which has electrodes at each end, one positive, one negative, connected to an external circuit. The slight but continuous radioactive bombardment strips electrons from some of the nitrogen atoms, and these free electrons move to the positive electrode – thus generating a steady electric current which can be monitored.

Now introduce a trace of a more chemically reactive gas, say DDT, into the stream of nitrogen.

This mops up some of the free electrons, and the current decreases. And it really only does need a trace to produce a detectable effect. A femtogram – a thousand million millionth of a gram – is enough to produce a reading.

While simple in principle, making and calibrating a working detector, and working out exactly what it is detecting, were anything but. As with many of Lovelock's inventions, it needed an unusual combination of theoretical understanding of atoms, molecules and electrons, intuitions about what that meant in practice, and a wealth of hands-on experience handling unusual substances, tuning electronic circuits, and generally being prepared to tinker purposefully without worrying too much about what the textbooks said. Bear in mind a few basic principles and parameters, then follow your nose, was Lovelock's method.

The reward was the satisfaction of making the thing work, but also much more. Although the ECD did not make money for its inventor directly – as Lovelock's autobiography relates, one of his spells working in the US eventually led to the patent being assigned to the US Government – being expert in its use was still immensely valuable. It was the kind of thing which gave entry to labs around the world, so that when he was on the trail of Gaia Lovelock could trade his advice on instruments for the chance to pick the brains of scientists from a whole range of disciplines. Devices like this had an industrial pay-off too, and even without a patent, companies were prepared to pay for Lovelock's expertise. By the early 1960s, he was ready to quit what had become a comfortable career in a Government institute and reinvent himself as a freelance, an independent scientist. After his crucial spells working for NASA, and other visits to American universities, he came back to the UK in 1963 finally prepared to do just that.

And so he has worked ever since, first in the village of Bowerchalke in Wiltshire, then since 1977 at Coombe Mill in Devon. Sustained by consultancies from companies like Shell and Hewlett Packard, and the odd grant, he has maintained a private laboratory, and a deeply ambivalent attitude to established science. His final move to work as an independent was a huge decision – well up there with other mid-life crises. Although gentlemen of means had worked as self-supported researchers into the nineteenth century, independent science had virtually disappeared in the twentieth. The life he now envisaged seemed more like that of artists and novelists than scientists, who were everywhere bound to institutions.

What was more, he and his first wife had four children, one of whom needed special care and education after a traumatic birth. He had a secure job in a scientific system which had seen lavish increases in support ever since the Second World War. Yet he increasingly saw himself as constrained by his professional life. It was more than freedom of thought, and the urge to find space to think, which led him to become self-supporting. By his own account, he had never much enjoyed the day-to-day business of dealing with other people and organisations. But he naturally emphasised the chance to think unconventional thoughts when he described the attractions of independence, and has often written about how much better it is to be self-supporting than to be a conventional researcher, beholden to one paymaster and, worse, to a single discipline. Maybe there is something in this – Gaia is nothing if not multi-disciplinary. But it was the much larger number of more conventional scientists, working in research institutes and universities, who Lovelock would have to persuade if the radical ideas he was now developing were to make any real impression on the intellectual world.

Speaker for the lower orders

Gaia is a tough bitch ...

Lynn Margulis

In the late 1960s, James Lovelock was building his new career, and also developing his thoughts on a self-regulating Earth whenever he could. He tried the basic idea out on many people, including his Bowerchalke neighbour, the novelist William Golding. Hearing Lovelock expound his notions of cybernetics, geochemistry, self-regulation and planetary homeostasis, Golding told him he needed a simple term to encapsulate his idea and get people's attention. And he immediately proposed that he name the hypothesis after Gaia, the Greek goddess of the Earth. The name stuck.

Wider scientific contacts had more mixed results. Engineers and space scientists, used to ideas about feedback and control, sometimes understood what he was on about. Biologists were sceptical. But the composition of the atmosphere and surface temperatures were the province of Earth scientists, who on the whole were not so much sceptical as uninterested. Only a few had ever really considered biological effects on the make-up of the planet's surface, and the rest felt there was no problem describing the processes shaping rocks and atmosphere in terms of geochemistry. Put chemicals in contact with each other on a planet-sized assembly of matter, and they simply, slowly, reacted with one another according to their molecular characteristics and energy levels. No biological intervention was required.

Although Lovelock had learnt a good deal of biology in his days in a medical research institute, he really needed a professional biologist to help him refine his ideas about the living Earth. With hindsight, he needed a microbiologist, as microorganisms have always been the majority shareholders in life on the planet. And the one he found, Lynn Margulis, was probably the best collaborator he could have happened upon. Although she was one of those legions of scientists toiling in university departments, she was anything but conventional. She already had one radical theory under her belt, and was ready to embrace another as part of her still developing biological world-view.

Lynn Margulis was born in 1938, and discovered science as a teenage student at the University of Chicago. She had already shown her independence of mind by sneaking off to her preferred choice of

Figure 2. Lynn Margulis, Lovelock's closest
collaborator on the detailed workings of Gaia.

high school without telling her parents. Now,
as a 14-year-old university entrant in a special
programme for early starters, she began to realise

that it was scientific questions which engaged her mind the most. She was encouraged in this by a fellow student, the already charismatic Carl Sagan, whom she eventually married. But while Sagan may have been forward-looking in science, his views about a woman's duty to support her husband's career did not chime with Margulis' ideas of what she wanted to do in life. By the early 1960s she had acquired a master's degree in zoology and genetics, a PhD from Berkeley, two young children and a divorce from the workaholic astronomer. Unde-terred, she ploughed on in science, regarded by her peers as bright but intellectually unsound, and – rather like Lovelock – eventually won through to an established position and a host of professional honours. But she did it all inside the system, and ended up as a Distinguished Research Professor at the University of Massachusetts at Amherst.

Margulis' big idea developed from thinking about symbiosis, the apparently co-operative relation-ships between two organisms from which both benefit. A bee feeding on nectar and spreading the pollen it picks up in the process is a simple example. Margulis, though, was charting the myriad of more intimate symbiotic relationships between micro-organisms, most of which had never been studied, or even suspected. And in the mid-1960s she was deeply involved with the idea that symbiosis was a vital force in evolution. Specifically, she believed that some of the most important parts of the cells of higher organisms arose not through the one-step-at-a-time mutations assumed by standard Darwinian theory, but through acquisition of symbiotic bacteria by their ancestors. It is a startling thought, because it means, for example, that all the mitochondria – the energy-producing units or organelles – in your cells are descendants of ancient micro-organisms. They began as invading parasites and ended as obligatory members of a co-operative cellular household. Viewed through Margulis' spectacles, a human is an enormous, shambling colony of bacteria.

Margulis' marshalling of evidence in favour of microbial 'endosymbiosis' as the best way to account for the origins of the mitochondria, as well as the photosynthetic chloroplasts found in plant cells, helped produce one of the most important shifts in ideas in the recent history of biology. Her theory, once derided, is now the stuff of school-books. She is still working on convincing everyone else that a third component of more complex cells, the motors which power their movements, has bacterial origins, though traces of this are proving harder to recover. But her reputation is solid, crowned by the award of a National Medal for Science from then-President Clinton, and she is still promoting the creatures she has devoted her life to studying. As her university web page puts it, 'she personally represents 250 million species of non-human, mute microorganisms and their descendants'.

When Lovelock and Margulis began their collaboration, she was devoting most of her energies to defending her endosymbiotic theory, first stated in detail in a paper in the *Journal of Theoretical Biology* in 1967, and elaborated in 1970 in a lengthy book, *The Origin of Eukaryotic Cells*. The reception had been dauntingly critical. A relative newcomer, and a woman in a still deeply sexist profession, had to be unusually determined to carry on defending her position. Clever, combative, well-informed, and deeply committed to a controversial change in ideas, Margulis was an ideal tactical as well as intellectual sounding board for the equally radically-minded but retiring and conflict-hating Lovelock.

Lovelock's first encounter with Margulis in fact took place at a meeting in Princeton in 1968. They did not speak then, as she was busy acting as a rapporteur. Nevertheless, Lovelock, who found his ideas ill-received at this conference, suggests that the 'eminent professors expected young scientists like Lynn and me to be seen and not heard'. The remark reveals something about his self-image, if nothing else. Margulis was only 29, but had already published the main lines of her endosymbiotic theory in a major academic journal. Lovelock was almost 50, and still looking for the most effective way to develop and publicise his ideas.

Three years later they met again, at Margulis' behest. The origins of oxygen were crucial for her micro-level theories of evolution of cells with oxygen-burning mitochondria, and she became curious about the role of oxygen in the atmosphere. Relations with Sagan had improved somewhat, and she asked him who to turn to for advice. The astronomer suggested his former JPL colleague Lovelock as a man who had thought hard about atmospheres.

When Lovelock eventually took up an invitation to visit Margulis in Boston, in 1971, there was a meeting of minds. Aside from their shared interest in radical theories, and their quasi-outsider status, both were interested in the whole Earth, both open to ideas linking macro- and micro-scale events, both trying to piece together stories about things which happened thousands of millions of years ago using whatever evidence they could lay their hands on. Their speculations ranged over the whole biota, the totality of all the living species on Earth. Lovelock recalls, 'together we explored endlessly the possible systems involving the biota that could serve as Gaian regulators of climate and chemistry'.

What's new?

The idea that the Earth is alive is probably as old as humankind ...

James Lovelock

As their ideas about what Gaia might actually mean developed, the two main advocates of the hypothesis also swapped notions about who had been thinking along similar lines in the past. Strictly, none of this has any bearing on the logical status or experimental evaluation of a scientific theory. But new theories are defended with rhetoric as well as logic, and here history has its uses. Scientists who want their colleagues to make a new turn typically get historical in three ways. They can appeal to novelty, asserting that their ideas are without precedent and represent a complete revolution. This is the boldest ploy, usually with mixed results. It tends to appeal to a disaffected minority but alienate more conventionally-minded researchers. Or, the advocates can stress continuity, showing how their ideas follow on from past suggestions. This is also a mixed blessing. It appeals less to the self-image of iconoclasts, and may play into the hands of critics who take up the suggestion that nothing really new is going on. Finally, there is a hybrid claim. The thoughts are not new, but are a recovery of ideas once accepted by the wise, but lately unaccountably neglected. Things took a wrong turn somewhere, which must now be corrected. Or, more accommodatingly, the most recently dominant ideas were productive in their way but have now outlived their usefulness – time for a new synthesis.

Gaia, on the whole, has lent itself best to this last strategy. In one sense it is implied by the name. Invoking the Earth goddess immediately suggests that past cultures were comfortable with the idea that the Earth is alive. It is also easy to see the development of modern ideas about Gaia as the latest stage in a long interplay between conceptions of the world and the human or animal body. This analogy, between the macrocosm and the microcosm, has been a recurring motif in Western thought since the ancient Greeks, and has generated influences which have affected later scientific thought at different times in different ways. Sometimes it has been helpful to see the Earth as like the human body. At others, it has mattered more to see the human body as like the Earth.

In light of this tradition, it is not surprising that there are a host of more specific episodes in the history of ideas which can be cited as precedents for Gaia. Among those, old and not so old, who have been claimed as forerunners of Gaia have been figures as diverse as James Hutton, widely credited with being the founder of scientific geology at the end of the eighteenth century, the early twentieth-century Jesuit palaeontologist and theorist of cosmic evolution Teilhard de Chardin, and the later anthropologist and systems theorist Gregory Bateson. Just about the only writer to have toyed with the idea of a living Earth who has not been presented as a proto-Gaian is Sir Arthur Conan Doyle, who in one of his more memorable short stories, 'The Day the Earth Screamed', has the redoubtable Professor Challenger supervising an ultra-deep drilling rig, which provokes the reaction described in the title.

Aside from these, there are a number of biologists, ecologists and Earth scientists who have put forward ideas which bear some relation to Gaia. Let's look at some of these ideas in more detail, concentrating on the figures Lovelock and Margulis maintain are most important, before looking again at what may be new about their own ideas.

James Hutton is often mentioned, but need not detain us long. An Edinburgh farmer and intellectual, his influential Theory of the Earth was first published in 1788 in the *Transactions of the Royal Society of Edinburgh*. Hutton had been pondering the processes of weathering and erosion, the origins of soil, and the different types of rock visible on the Earth around him. He proposed to unite them all in a grand theory in which the Earth's internal heat produced upwellings of molten material, hence new surface rock. In time – and he was one of the first geologists to see time as effectively unlimited – the rock was weathered away, producing fresh soil which eventually washed into the seas as sediment. This sediment would, in turn, sink down, to be reheated and expand, perhaps returning one day to the surface.

Figure 3. James Hutton, pioneer geologist whose ideas pointed towards geophysiology.

This perfectly poised recycling thus renewed the landscape exploited by farmers like Hutton, and provided evidence for the good intentions of the Creator. But although the rocks in Hutton's theory undergo a kind of metabolism, there is no role for living things in his Earth system, except for the plants which trap sunlight and lay down the enormous stores of fuel which he believed generate the subterranean heat. He was, though, strongly influenced by the macrocosm–microcosm analogy. As a medical student he wrote an MD thesis on the circulation of the blood, and he saw the circulation of matter in the Earth as essentially similar. As he put it: 'We are thus led to see a circulation in the matter of this globe, and a beautiful economy in the works of nature. This earth, like the body of an animal, is wasted at the same time that it is repaired.'

The reason why Lovelock is especially keen on having Hutton as a forebear, however, is that the pioneering geologist took the analogy one step further, and suggested that the proper study of the Earth would be a kind of physiology. As Lovelock was toying with the notion of geophysiology (of which more later), he was much taken with this proposal and mentioned it at every opportunity. If a man celebrated as a founder of a new scientific discipline had employed such terms, surely Lovelock could use the precedent to add weight to his own claims? There is no reason to think, though, that Hutton believed the Earth was alive. Although he was fluent in the language fit for comparing macrocosm and microcosm, for him it was strictly an analogy, an argument from correspondence, not an identity. In fact, he referred to an 'earth machine'. His theory did not need the Earth to be alive any more than does the currently accepted theory of rock circulation, through movement of tectonic plates and generation and removal of rock at plate boundaries. Convection currents, albeit unusually large ones now powered by radioactive heat, do all the work both for Hutton and for modern geologists. (There have been some speculations that Gaia gets involved in plate tectonics, too, but we won't go into that here.)

The microcosm–macrocosm analogy, then, is suggestive, but does not lead directly to Gaia. It is still appealing, though, to recall its role in key pieces of past scientific thinking. One of Lovelock and Margulis' earliest statements of the hypothesis recalled that William Harvey's idea of the circulation of the blood was partly inspired by Aristotle's much older notion of the weather cycle. This developed into a picture of evaporation, condensation, rainfall and run-off back into the sea which we still recognise as the basis for movement of water between land, sea and air. The idea of chemical, and geochemical, and then biogeochemical cycles is

Figure 4. One step in a long tradition: a seventeenth-century version of the macrocosm–microcosm metaphor, likening the circulation of the blood to the cycles of weather.

certainly crucial to Gaian science, and to Earth system science more generally. On the other hand, the general idea of a cycle – circulation of matter, and cyclical processes – is now such a common feature of scientific theories that it hardly needs specific precedent to account for its appearance.

There are a number of more specific precedents for ideas about close links between life and its environment. They include work by the pioneer twentieth-century population biologist Alfred Lotka, who in the 1920s argued that study of evolution of organisms ought to take into account evolution of their environments. G.E. Hutchinson of Yale University pointed out that the Earth's atmosphere was a chemical anomaly, but was disinclined to speculate about why this should be so. And the ecologist Eugene Odum presented ideas about feedback controls in ecological systems which anticipated on a smaller scale what Lovelock proposed globally.

But perhaps the most impressive candidate for an early stab at what we may now see as Gaian thinking is the Russian Earth scientist Vladimir Vernadsky and his expansive conception of the biosphere. The term was originally coined casually by the Austrian geologist Edward Suess, who used it in a book on the Alps. For Suess, the biosphere was a layer on and above the Earth's surface where life is found – the analogy was with concentric layers of the atmosphere like the stratosphere and the troposphere.

According to historian Jacques Grinevald, it was

Vernadsky who first used the term in its modern sense, most notably in his pioneering essay on *The Biosphere*, first published in 1926. But the author, who was born in 1863, had been developing his dynamic, integrated view of the planet for some decades. His view of the Earth in this prescient, book-length account is replete with arguments which anticipate the picture Lovelock and Margulis wanted to draw in the 1970s. Essentially, he promoted the biosphere as a way of emphasising that life as a whole influenced geology as well as being influenced by it. 'Among numerous works on geology', he wrote in his preface, 'none has adequately treated the biosphere as a whole, and none viewed it, as it will be viewed here, as a single orderly manifestation of the mechanism of the uppermost region of the planet – the Earth's crust'.

For Vernadsky, 'Living matter gives the biosphere an extraordinary character ... Two distinct types of matter, inert and living, though separated by the impassable gulf of their geological history, exert a reciprocal action upon one another.' And his view of this action was influenced by just the kind of thermodynamic considerations which would preoccupy Lovelock when he came to ponder the characteristics of life. Above all, the biosphere was 'a region of transformers that convert cosmic radiations into active energy in electrical, mechanical, thermal, and other forms ... It is living matter – the Earth's total sum of living organisms – that transforms the radiant energy of the sun into the active chemical energy of the biosphere.'

There followed a series of calculations which tried to show what quantities of various chemicals might be transformed by the living material of the Earth taken as a whole. The details of these often go awry, according to more up-to-date estimates, but the general approach is what is important. Again, there are clear similarities with the broad-brush figuring which Lovelock would offer in his books and papers, and the more detailed work which would follow.

There are, of course, differences. Vernadsky did not regard the Earth itself as alive, and, as Lovelock wrote, 'did not seem to have a feeling for system science and the tight-coupled feedback between life and its environment'. In fact, he disagreed with Margulis about Vernadsky's importance, although he glossed over this in his writing in the 1980s, in which he was considerably more enthusiastic about the Russian's significance as a pioneer of Gaian thinking.

Figure 5. Vladimir Vernadsky. The dilapidation of the statue is a faithful reflection of his status as a little-recognised pioneer of Earth systems thinking.

More importantly, perhaps, Vernadsky was entirely unknown to both Lovelock and Margulis when they pursued their first discussions of Gaia. Although he was celebrated in the former Soviet

Union, his work was little read in the West, as it remained confined to Russian texts and to an early French translation. A complete English language edition of *The Biosphere* did not appear until 1998, more than half a century after Vernadsky's death, more than thirty years after the first glimmerings of Gaia.

The whole Earth gallery

The start of the Gaia hypothesis was the view of the Earth from space, revealing the planet as a whole but not in detail.

James Lovelock

The ideas of Hutton, Vernadsky and the others were thus useful to Lovelock in his efforts to promote his vision of a science of the whole Earth. But these putative scientific forerunners of Gaia offered little in the way of direct influences on Lovelock's first formulations. For the most part he had simply never heard of them then. But there were certainly more diffuse cultural influences which everybody knew about. One which he cites himself is the new image of Earth delivered by the space programme. Astronauts on early orbital flights repeatedly testified to the emotional power of seeing the Earth from their new vantage point (Shuttle crew still do). When the Apollo programme sent men to the moon, the colour pictures of the home planet that they brought back had enormous impact. So as well as the formal discussion of planets and how they are built which marked Lovelock's time at NASA, the image of Spaceship Earth, the phrase coined by the visionary architect Buckminster Fuller, seized the imagination. Whether isolated against the darkness of space or rising luminous above the all-too-dead moonscape, the swirling blue planet encouraged the idea that Earth's systems were all part of one entity.

The image was and remains important, for who can resist its beauty? But the full story of Spaceship Earth is more complicated – in two ways. First, the original idea was pretty mechanistic. Buckminster Fuller's influential book of 1963 betrayed this in its title: *An Operating Manual for Spaceship Earth*. As Lovelock was to point out, one implication of the idea of Earth as a spaceship was that it carried a crew who were in charge of the vessel and knew how to fly it. His view was quite different – that Earth would get along quite well without us, and notions that we could take responsibility for 'operating' it were sheer hubris.

Even so, other aspects of the idea pointed towards a closer investigation of the processes which kept the ship habitable. As economist and social philosopher Kenneth Boulding put it in an address in 1965:

Once we begin to look at earth as a space ship, the appalling extent of our ignorance about it is almost frightening. This is true of the level of every science. We know practically nothing, for instance, about the long-run dynamics even of the physical system of the earth. We do not understand, for instance, the machinery of ice ages, the real nature of geological stability or disturbance, the incidence of volcanism and earthquakes, and we understand fantastically little about that enormously complex heat engine known as the atmosphere. We do not even know whether the activities of man are going to make the earth warm up or cool off.

The second complication in the story is the power ascribed to images from space. The planetary consciousness which began to influence many people in the 1960s was surely enhanced by the Earthrise posters blu-tacked to a million walls. Yet its significance was realised in the imagination well ahead of real photographs. It was realised by Vernadsky, for example, who wrote long before any such image existed that:

*The face of the Earth viewed from celestial space presents a unique appearance, different from all other heavenly bodies. The surface that separates the planet from the cosmic medium is the **biosphere**, visible principally because of light from the sun.* [Original emphasis]

The imaginative journey Vernadsky invited his reader to make was prefigured, in turn, by Suess – the originator of the term 'biosphere' – who on the first page of his influential turn-of-the-twentieth-century geological overview of *The Face of the Earth* suggested that:

[W]*e imagine an observer to approach our planet from outer space, and, pushing aside the belts of red-brown clouds which obscure our atmosphere, to gaze for a whole day on the surface of the earth as it rotates beneath him ...*

Later in the twentieth century, there were artistic efforts to depict the image of the Earth from space based on improved astronomical understanding. Real, technically grounded space programmes have always been closely intertwined with imaginary ones, and never more so than in the career of the celebrated American painter Chesley Bonestell. He began selling views of the other planets with a famous image of 'Saturn as Seen from Titan' which appeared in *Life* magazine in 1944, and he went on to work with astronomers, rocket designers and space scientists to paint hundreds of pictures which presented views of other worlds so convincing that it seemed almost as if the real space programme had already explored the farthest reaches of the Solar System. When film producer George Pal made *Destination Moon* a few years later, Bonestell, who had already worked extensively in Hollywood, was signed up to ensure that the view of the Earth in the lunar sky was scientifically accurate. The result was a special effects Oscar for Pal and another striking addition to the culture's growing familiarity with the notion that the Earth seen from space would be special. By the 1960s, some environmentalists were so taken with the potential of Earth images for transforming consciousness that they became impatient for NASA – which began operation in 1958 – to deliver the real thing. In 1966, the cultural entrepreneur Stuart Brand was selling badges asking: 'Why Haven't We Seen a Photograph of the Whole Earth Yet?'

Today, when NASA's databases give web access to hundreds of thousands of Earth images, their cumulative impact would be an interesting historical

Figure 6. One of a kind? Spaceship Earth – as finally revealed to her inhabitants by NASA.

study. But the, as it were, pre-history of Spaceship Earth suggests that it was not simply the new photos of our planetary home which account for a shift in perception, or for Gaia theory. The change in cultural consciousness which they helped to amplify was already well under way before a 'world view' completed its shift from being a purely metaphorical to a literal notion.

The significance of the image was also realised by at least one of the twentieth century's most powerful writers. We know that Lovelock had a youthful taste for science books, but also for science fiction – by the pioneers of the genre, H.G. Wells and Jules Verne, and by a new writer, the great visionary Englishman Olaf Stapledon. He has never cited it as an inspiration, but a passage early in Stapledon's finest book, *Star Maker*, sounds suggestive, to say the least. The narrator, who will voyage to the far reaches of the Universe in an unexplained flight of imagination, has just departed from Earth and, in his far-seeing mind's eye, he looks back:

The spectacle before me was strangely moving. Personal anxiety was blotted out by wonder and admiration; for the sheer beauty of our planet

surprised me. It was a huge pearl, set in spangled
ebony. It was nacreous, it was an opal. No, it was
far more lovely than any jewel. Its patterned
colouring was more subtle, more ethereal. It
displayed the delicacy and brilliance, the intricacy
and harmony, of a live thing. Strange that in my
remoteness I seemed to feel, as never before, the
vital presence of Earth as a creature alive but
tranced and obscurely yearning to wake.

Star Maker cannot have been one of the novels
which the schoolboy Lovelock borrowed from
Brixton Library, as it was not published until 1937.
But as a Stapledon reader, it is hard to imagine that
he did not get hold of it when it did appear. Perhaps
photographs taken from orbiting NASA spacecraft
sound a more respectable influence than cosmic
fictions?

· CHAPTER III ·

GOING PUBLIC

The Gaia hypothesis is for those who like to walk or simply stand and stare, to wonder about the Earth and the life it bears, and to speculate about the consequences of our own presence here.

James Lovelock

A scientist with a new idea is supposed to write a paper for a professional journal laying out the argument and the evidence which might support it and, ideally, how it might be tested by getting more evidence. The paper is then sent to others in the field for peer review and comment, and recommended for publication if they think it is good enough. This system has a lot going for it. It provides quality control and makes sure that new knowledge builds from what is already known, or contradicts it only with good reason. But it was never likely to work for Gaia. Peer review easily tends to conservatism. The sensible assumption that extraordinary claims demand extraordinary evidence can turn into scepticism about all novelties. Less defensibly, it locks scientists into recognised patterns of expertise and understanding, usually deeply rooted in one corner of a single discipline. A notion like Gaia, which was deliberately cast in terms which questioned established disciplinary boundaries, was always going to have a hard time in the professional literature. Problems such as which journals, in what field, and who would understand what was being said well enough to pass a considered opinion, meant that conventional paths to publication were almost impossible to follow. Lovelock managed to get a one-page statement of the basic ideas, which began as a short conference talk, published in the journal *Atmospheric Environment* in 1972, and Lovelock and Margulis published two brief papers in the less mainstream journals *Tellus* and *Icarus*, the latter then edited by Carl Sagan, a couple of years later. But none of these made much of a dent in wider opinion.

There is an alternative, riskier, way of promoting heterodox scientific ideas – to write directly for the public. Once this was a pretty standard way of doing the job, as Charles Darwin might testify. But now that formal scientific publication is so much more specialised, launching new ideas in a book aimed at

Figure 7. Carl Sagan, planetary scientist who helped usher *Gaia* into print.

the general reader is usually frowned upon as the province of the flaky or the cranky, of those who are not writing science, but writing their way out of science. The biologist Rupert Sheldrake, for example, outlined his extremely unconventional notions about embryonic development in a book for the general reader, *A New Science of Life*, in 1981. As they entailed belief in a whole set of things hitherto unsuspected by scientists, including 'morphic resonance' in a so-called 'morphogenetic field', and harked back frankly to a brand of vitalism which virtually all working biologists repudiated, the reaction was mostly derision. But there were even more hostile scientific responses, epitomised by the suggestion from the then editor of the influential journal *Nature* that it was 'a book fit for burning'. This did no harm to the book's sales – Sheldrake has quoted it ever since. But it helped to destroy his chances of being taken seriously again as a scientist. Sheldrake is still writing, and has a minor cult following, but has about as much influence on mainstream science as, say, Uri Geller. Even biologists with different, heterodox ideas about development go to great lengths to dissociate themselves from his ideas. Anyone who wrote a popular book claiming that the Earth was alive undoubtedly risked similar treatment.

Nevertheless, this was the next important development in the history of Gaia. It was triggered by an article Lovelock co-wrote in the British magazine *New Scientist* in 1975, called 'The Quest for Gaia'. Scientists may be wary of the search for the next 'big idea', but publishers know a good thing when they see one, and he immediately had more than twenty approaches to write a book giving all the details. For a man who had once thought that his life as an independent scientist might be supported by writing science fiction, it was not an invitation to resist. The first edition of *Gaia: A New Look at Life on Earth* appeared from the prestigious Oxford University Press in 1979, the first of three full-length books that Lovelock was to write expounding Gaian ideas. It demands a detailed look. It was the book that first introduced the thinking behind Gaia to a wide audience, scientific and non-scientific, and it drew reactions which powerfully influenced the history of Gaia over the next quarter-century.

Gaia – A New Look at Life on Earth

The book begins with a reference to NASA's Viking landings on Mars as a search for life, and tells us that that is also Lovelock's subject: '[T]he quest for Gaia is an attempt to find the largest living creature on Earth.' There follows a first, general statement of the Gaia hypothesis as proposing an entity which is more than the sum of its parts:

> *Our journey may reveal no more than the almost infinite variety of living forms which have proliferated over the Earth's surface under the transparent case of the air and which constitute the biosphere. But if Gaia does exist, then we may find ourselves and all other living things to be parts and partners of a vast being who in her entirety has the power to maintain our planet as a fit and comfortable habitat for life.*

In this first paragraph, we already have a choice example of the kind of rhetoric which would alarm the referees of a scientific paper. There is the personification of Gaia, perhaps the gender too, the suggestion that 'we' are part of something much larger than ourselves, and the implication of agency – Gaia has the power. It is not, strictly, religious language, but it comes close. As an alternative, a little later the idea is presented as mere common sense, among those in touch with the realities of life:

> *Scientists are usually condemned to lead urban lives, but I find that country people still living*

close to the earth often seem puzzled that anyone
should need to make a formal proposition of
anything as obvious as the Gaia hypothesis. For
them it is true and always has been.

This opposition between country and city became
another of Lovelock's regular motifs. Years later, he
was still emphasising that 'urban life alienates us
from Gaia'. At the same time, he always insisted
that Gaia was a scientific hypothesis and should be
evaluated as such.

In the book, Lovelock then relates his involvement with NASA's life detection programme, the
difficulty of defining life, and the idea that entropy
reduction is the key sign to look for, as I described
earlier. From this, it seemed that the decrease of
entropy, or the persistent chemical disequilibrium,
in Earth's atmosphere was a clear sign of biological
activity. In his first example, the normal rate of
reaction between methane and oxygen in sunlight
means that at least a billion tons of methane must
enter the atmosphere every year to maintain the
observed levels of the gas, together with twice the
quantity of oxygen. 'The quantities of both these
gases required to keep the Earth's extraordinary
atmospheric mixture constant was improbable on

an abiological basis by at least 100 orders of magnitude', he concludes.

Then he tells how, a few years later, after working extensively on atmospheric pollution for Shell, this first realisation of the importance of life had blossomed into the full Gaia hypothesis, which embraces more than the biosphere. Gaia is now 'a complex entity involving the Earth's biosphere, atmosphere, oceans and soil; the totality consti- tuting a feedback or cybernetic system which seeks an optimal physical and chemical environment for life on this planet'. Note that 'optimal', which was to cause no end of trouble.

The next chapter relates the 4,500-million-year history of the Earth, emphasising the many ways in which the development of the biosphere could have stalled after the first emergence of life. Some- how, a series of potentially terminal crises must have been dealt with. It is easy to imagine small changes in atmospheric composition, absorption or reflection of solar radiation, depletion or excess of particular chemicals, which would have produced conditions which all the kinds of life we know would have found intolerable. The advent of large amounts of atmospheric oxygen, around two billion years ago, itself a result of the appearance of new kinds of organisms, was a final serious threat to earlier kinds of life, for whom oxygen was (and still is) poisonous – Lynn Margulis calls the resulting loss of many species the 'oxygen holocaust'.

How, then, did life manage to survive all these perils? Answer: by developing the interactions which are the mark of Gaia. As Lovelock summed up this whole perilous history:

The first appearance of oxygen in the air heralded an almost fatal catastrophe for early life. To have avoided by blind chance death from freezing or boiling, from starvation, acidity, or grave metabolic disturbance, and finally from poisoning, seems too much to ask; but if the early biosphere was already evolving into much more than just a catalogue of species and was assuming the capacity for planetary control, our survival through those hazardous times is less difficult to comprehend.

There's another interesting touch here. The 'we' of the introduction presumably refers to readers, or humans in general. But this whole chapter is concerned with events aeons before humans appeared, so 'our survival' must refer to life as a whole. Lovelock's protagonist, with whom the reader is here invited to identify, is now the entire biosphere. This, though, is just the kind of thing which would irk some of his sternest critics, the strict Darwinians.

After this short evolutionary story, or perhaps fable, the following chapters fill out the picture of Gaia. They include a more systematic look at all the signs of entropy reduction which a theory of the Earth might need to account for. Lovelock compares what is known about the Martian and Venusian atmospheres with a hypothetical non-living Earth in chemical equilibrium. Again he drives home the point that the composition of Earth's atmosphere is highly improbable. Not just oxygen, but nitrogen, carbon dioxide, methane, ammonia, even argon, are present in anomalous amounts, but amounts which suit the ensemble of living things remarkably well. For example, Lovelock reports recent (in 1979) experiments which suggested that, while oxygen is vital for respiration, taking the atmospheric levels just a few per cent above the 21 per cent found naturally would allow even damp wood to burn. In such an atmosphere, a single lightning strike would ignite an unstoppable orgy of chemical combination, a conflagration which would consume all the world's forests.

Figure 8. Forest fire. If this is what happens with 21 per cent of atmospheric oxygen, better not increase it.

The atmosphere, as ever, is thus a prime Gaian exhibit. But the book presents others. The chemistry of the seas is also important, with both acidity and salt content staying in a range hospitable to life. More than 500 million tons of salt is washed from land into the sea every year, an amount which would take all the oceans to their current level of salinity in around 80 million years. Something keeps them from getting saltier than their present 3.4 per cent concentration, however, which is just as well, as anything above 6 per cent kills most known organisms. And there is the large question of global temperature, which Lovelock suggests has stayed between 10 and 20 degrees centigrade for the past three billion years in the face of a range of potentially disturbing influences. As with any new explanatory theory, the author has to persuade readers that there are things which need explaining. Gaia, it is suggested, explains quite a lot.

In the midst of this, Lovelock offers a brief introduction to ideas about feedback and control drawn from cybernetics, and how they can be used to describe the regulation of systems in individual living organisms. After describing the classic example of a thermostatically controlled oven, he writes that 'the key to understanding cybernetic systems is that, like life itself, they are always more than the mere assembly of constituent parts'.

There is then a quite detailed discussion of one aspect of human physiology, the regulation of body temperature. This is achieved by a combination of things – shivering, sweating, and dilating or constricting blood vessels as well as chemical heat production – all responding to internal and external signals. As Lovelock relates, this kind of bodily co-ordination led the American Walter Cannon in the 1930s to coin a key term, homeostasis, for the processes which maintain a steady state in a living system. This, he suggests, is what we will be trying to unravel on a planetary scale if we wish to uncover the mechanisms through which Gaia operates.

The analogy with human physiology – the microcosm–macrocosm link again – was one which Lovelock and others would develop much more extensively in years to come, but it is already quite explicit in his first extended look at Gaia. And it is used to help think about function as well as mechanism. Considering all those oddly balanced gases, for instance, he writes:

> We shall ... examine the atmosphere in much the same way that a physiologist might examine the contents of the blood, to see what function it serves in maintaining the living creature of which it is a part.

Much of his discussion is taken up with new descriptions of facts already known, but one story that Lovelock tells is offered as a prediction inspired by Gaian thinking which has been borne out. It was a prediction which marked the start of one of the most fruitful lines of research which can be traced back to Gaia, and one I shall return to several times to help show how the science has developed.

It concerns an element not yet mentioned here: sulphur.

The first Gaian notions about sulphur are a good example of Lovelock's thinking at the time, and are appreciably simpler than the research which came later. There is a cycling of sulphur in the environment, as there is for many other substances, and conventional understanding seemed recently to have revealed a 'sulphur gap'. Measurements of the weathering of sulphur-bearing rocks, sulphur take-up by plants, and of gaseous sulphur compounds dumped into the atmosphere by burning coal and oil seemed to add up to less sulphur in total than was being carried down to the sea by the action of rivers. Some unknown carrier must be transporting sulphur dissolved in the ocean back to land. But what?

The best suggestion around in the late 1960s was that it might be hydrogen sulphide. But there were doubts about this on chemical grounds, and very little is present in the atmosphere. Lovelock bet on another sulphur compound, dimethyl sulphide, knowing that there are marine algae which stick methyl groups ($CH3$) onto sulphur, perhaps as a means of getting rid of an unwanted chemical by turning it into something more volatile.

Sounds reasonable. But a proposal to the British Natural Environment Research Council to test it during passage on their ocean-going research vessel HMS *Shackleton* was unanimously rejected by the committee handing out grants. In what became one of Lovelock's favourite small stories against the peer review system, this is said to have been because a chemist on the committee refused to believe that chlorofluorocarbons, which Lovelock also proposed to measure on the voyage, could be detected at the levels he predicted would be dispersed in the atmosphere. These man-made chemicals, the CFCs, turned out to be the ozone-eaters which caused such concern to governments as well as environmentalists a few years later, but that is an episode largely separate from the history of Gaia theory. At any rate, 'this was to be the last occasion that I applied for research funds through the regular system of writing a proposal and submitting it to a funding agency', Lovelock wrote later.

Measuring very small quantities, of course, was Lovelock's speciality, and the civil servants who ran the Research Council realised this. Unusually, they offered Lovelock free passage on the ship, provided he paid for his own instruments, and he agreed. On the voyage, dimethyl sulphide (DMS) did indeed prove to be present throughout the oceans. At the time that the first Gaia book was written, other scientists had suggested that the amounts in mid-ocean were still not adequate to bridge the sulphur gap. Lovelock, in turn, proposed that much more DMS was produced in inshore waters by algal seaweeds. His conclusion in 1979 was that 'the biological methylation of sulphur appears to be Gaia's way of ensuring a proper balance between the sulphur in the sea and on land'.

That pretty much summed up the state of the evidence for Gaia in the first hundred or so pages of the first book. There were some features of the Earth which seemed hard to account for. They appeared to be related to the action of living organisms. Add all those actions together, and they showed the totality of life working, as it were, for the common good. And, although Lovelock would later work much harder to avoid such language, Gaia was quite often depicted as a creature with intentions and goals. As well as balancing sulphur, for example, she showed 'impatience with the leisurely progress towards equilibrium in the case of carbon dioxide'. In some sense, Gaia was running the show. And while the core of the book presented what was styled as a hypothesis, the introduction and the two closing chapters made it sound more like a world-view. How would the world react?

Finding readers

> *It was and still sometimes is difficult for trained evolutionists to refrain from regarding Gaia as the latest deification of the Earth by nature nuts …*
>
> Lynn Margulis and Dorion Sagan

For a small book, *Gaia* drew a big reaction. But the reactions were mixed, to say the least. Several non-scientific publics took the book to heart. Here was a new way of looking at things. It spoke to those with a new-found concern for the environment. It even seemed to offer some semblance of religious feeling in an increasingly secular age. There was nothing so old-fashioned as God in Lovelock's vision, but the self-organising principle of Gaia seemed to some to have God-like powers. At the very least, it made the Universe sound *hospitable*. This was pretty much the author's own position. Just a couple of years before, the physicist Steven Weinberg had summed up his interpretation of the scientific world-view of modern cosmology in his popular book about the

Big Bang, *The First Three Minutes*: '[T]he more the universe seems comprehensible, the more it also seems pointless.' Lovelock presented Gaia as 'an alternative to that ... depressing picture of our planet as a demented spaceship, forever travelling, driverless and purposeless, around an inner circle of the sun'. He never said quite what the purpose might be, so readers were free to fill in the blanks.

Scientists, though, were less beguiled by this hypothesis named after a Greek goddess. A few scientific reviewers were enthusiastic – including agricultural scientist Kenneth Mellanby in *New Scientist*, microbiologist Rene Dubos in *Nature* and physicist Phillip Morrison in *Scientific American*. But they were exceptions. Geologists, in the main, found the ideas it led to unnecessary. They believed that they could account for the history of the atmosphere through conventional geochemistry. Biologists were harsher. Some of them felt that there was something objectionable about this planetary conspiracy to keep things cosy. They had been raised on the idea of Nature red in tooth and claw. They weren't about to let it go on the basis of some speculations about atmospheric chemistry, especially when they came from a man who built clever instruments but sounded one minute like a regular scientist, the next like someone celebrating the wisdom of the tribal elders.

Objections to a living Earth

The sharpest criticisms of Gaia came from leading Darwinian theorists. The two most acute critiques, from the English populariser of the 'selfish' gene Richard Dawkins and the American W. Ford Doolittle, asked a hard question. Where was the pay-off for the individual organism helping to regulate the planet? Both wanted to know how it could possibly make sense for large or small features of Gaia to be linked to natural selection, which is the only way we know for evolution to proceed. And they questioned the co-operative emphasis of Lovelock's hypothesis. This aspect of Gaia, which was exactly what had appealed to Lynn Margulis, was out of line with the ruthless competition which drove natural selection, they believed.

Ironically, Dawkins' most widely read comment on Gaia came in his book *The Extended Phenotype*, first published in 1982, in which he argues brilliantly that genes *can* have an effect beyond the bounds of the organism which bears them. But not nearly as far as the Gaia hypothesis would suggest.

The furthest action at a distance he can think of, he suggests, is several miles – the distance between the far shore of a beaver lake and the beaver genes whose survival chances the lake increases.

When it came to Gaia, Dawkins was dismissive. 'The fatal flaw in Lovelock's hypothesis would have instantly occurred to him if he had wondered about the level of natural selection process which would be required in order to produce the Earth's supposed adaptation.' That is, the level of whole planets. So in Dawkins' view, for Gaia to evolve, there would need to be a host of planets all with biospheres with more or less efficient homeostasis. 'The Universe would have to be full of dead planets whose homeostatic regulation systems had failed, with, dotted around, a handful of successful, well-regulated planets of which Earth is one.' Even if this seems more likely today, when extra-solar planets seem to be reported by astronomers almost daily, Dawkins still has a clinching point. Such planetary systems would need to be able to reproduce, the more successful ones increasing in number, the less successful dying off. Only thus could natural selection occur.

For Dawkins, the existence of Gaia must imply natural selection on this cosmic scale. His version of

Darwinism had scored tremendous explanatory success working from the assumption that the units of selection are individual genes. He was resolutely opposed to the idea that selection at higher levels – the species or the ecosystem, for example – had any appreciable effects. From his standpoint, Gaia seemed like so-called 'group selection' taken to a ridiculous extreme. His view of the operation of Darwinian selection on a single planet made it virtually impossible to see how so many organisms would ever end up acting for the greater good – and he believed Lovelock ignored this problem. He called Gaia an extreme form of the 'BBC theorem', a splendid jibe at old natural history films with commentaries rhapsodising about the harmony of the natural world. But his real target was pop-ecology, with its emphasis on connectedness and a richly woven web maintaining a balance of nature. If nature is balanced for a strict Darwinian, it is a balance between essentially hostile forces, constantly probing for chinks in one another's armour or, more generally, looking for a larger share of limited resources. They can have no interest in maintaining an optimal environment for life in general, only for organisms-in-particular.

Doolittle's critique is similar, but probably made more of an impression on Lovelock by appearing earlier, and in a journal in which he might have looked for a more sympathetic hearing, Stewart Brand's eco-friendly *Co-Evolution Quarterly*. He certainly pulled no punches in his introduction:

> *The good thing about this engaging little book by Jim Lovelock is that reading it gives one a warm, comforting feeling about Nature and Man's place in it. The bad thing is that this feeling is based on a view of natural selection – that force which alone is responsible for the existence and characteristics of the biosphere – which is unquestionably false.*

Here is the hard-nosed scientist about to dip the musings of a well-meaning but unconvincing thinker into an acid bath of rigour. As he goes through the arguments, Doolittle has two main criticisms. Gaia must have the capacity to modify the environment – increasing the amount of sunlight reflected from the Earth to regulate temperature, for example. Then there must also be sensors, like those in any cybernetic system, which provide the information needed to tune the various features under Gaian control to achieve homeostasis. Lovelock says they are there, but mostly fails to identify them.

Of course, the fact that the mechanisms which would need to operate for Gaia to have, say, a thermostat, have not yet been identified does not mean that new research might not reveal some of them. But it is Doolittle's second, stronger criticism which is rammed home most forcefully. 'It is not the difficulty of unravelling Gaian feedback loops that makes me doubt her existence. It is the impossibility of imagining *any* evolutionary mechanisms by which these loops could have arisen or now be maintained.'

Just as Dawkins makes fun of the BBC theorem, Doolittle uses his near-namesake Dr Dolittle to ridicule Lovelock's conception of nature. Specifically, he recalls that in *Dr Dolittle on the Moon* the visitor finds that moon creatures manage without Darwinian competition thanks to the oversight of 'The Lunar Council'. This Council has members from the animal and vegetable kingdoms, and regulates the affairs of all so well that warfare is obsolete. Lovelock's Gaia is the terrestrial equivalent of the Lunar Council, Doolittle writes. 'But the Council was created by Otho Bludge, the first moon man and a refugee from Earth. Who created Gaia?'

Certainly not natural selection, in his view. This could happen only if organisms which behaved in such a way as to contribute to the maintenance of Gaia increased their own chances of leaving offspring compared with those which did not. This strict Darwinian framework can accommodate symbiosis, even whole ecosystems, where the organisms are in intimate contact. But not something as grand and long-lasting as Gaia. In reproductive terms, the distance and timescales involved mean that:

[T]*he rewards for good (Gaian) behaviour are as remote as the penalties for bad behaviour. It is difficult to accept that behaviours whose effects on atmospheric or oceanic composition or global temperature will not be felt for thousands of generations can be selected for, especially when the first beneficiaries of those effects may be organisms which are not themselves responsible for them.*

This was damning stuff, and Lovelock's first reaction, he wrote years later, 'was shock and incoherent disbelief'. As well as being stung by the charges of inconsistency and logical fallacy which

Doolittle laid, he must surely also have been pained by the paper's closing suggestion that the effect of his ideas would be ecologically harmful. People would think they could abuse the environment and Gaia would set things right. The reality, Doolittle assured the environmentally concerned readers of the *Co-Evolution Quarterly*, was much more likely to be that if the feedbacks Lovelock sought existed, then they were a matter of chance, and might easily be disturbed. An accidental system was inherently fragile, and so needed all the protection from environmentalists it could get.

Lovelock's first worked-out response, printed alongside Doolittle's review, was brief, and suggested that the fact that life modifies its environment constrains evolutionary developments in ways which make it more likely that feedback loops will close. Lynn Margulis, who also replied immediately, made the rather disingenuous comment that Doolittle was wrong to suggest that natural selection alone is responsible for shaping life: 'Single factor hypotheses of the evolutionary process went out with the 19th century.' Real Darwinian theory, she said, unites three things – accurate replication, inherited variation, *and* natural selection. It seems a little odd to point this out, partly because every professional biologist regards it as an elementary truth, partly because it does not really affect Doolittle's argument. Nevertheless, she concluded that: 'Taken together the evolutionary process does explain the emergence of Gaia as a control system, although admittedly many detailed mechanisms – indeed most – remain to be explained.'

In other writings, Margulis would say much more about the limitations of some interpretations of evolutionary theory, seen from the perspective of her ever-growing appreciation of the co-operative powers of micro-organisms. But here she concedes what she and Lovelock must both have realised on studying these critiques. *Gaia* as a book-length statement of the Gaia hypothesis was only a beginning. There was much more work to do.

With friends like these …

While the two main architects of Gaia theory got on with refining their ideas and trying to see their way around these scientific objections, the warm reception for their ideas outside science broadened and deepened. Lovelock corresponded with religious thinkers, and developed his own gentle brand of agnostic nature worship. Margulis was sometimes sharper with 'new age' responses to Gaia, but recognised that the idea had a mythological as well as a scientific resonance.

Many writers and activists, though, took the idea further than either of its originators might have imagined. Detailing all the turns that Gaia has taken in the wider culture would take a long book, and involve extensive research on the wilder shores of the world wide web in pursuit of votaries of the Earth goddess. But it is worth looking at a couple of examples of writers who see themselves as taking science itself in new, more spiritual, directions, and who have taken up Gaia for their own purposes.

The first is Fritjof Capra, a former physicist who has devoted a whole career to promoting cultural change through reinterpreting science. He first came to fame in the 1970s with his book *The Tao of Physics*. This struck a chord with many in the contemporary 'counter-culture' by arguing that the relativistic, indeterminist physics of the twentieth century was a recovery of ancient mystical wisdom. The implication of the observer in the observed, quantum entanglements leading to action at a distance, the uncertainty principle: none of these, he suggested, would come as any surprise to pre-scientific thinkers with non-mechanistic world-views. Therefore – and he did press this apparent homology into an argument, albeit a pretty dodgy one – modern physics validated the turn to old beliefs.

His next book, *The Turning Point* (1982), was more ambitious, bringing together a vast catalogue of ideas in support of a single overarching thesis – that the 'rising culture' which Capra discerned in the varied social, intellectual and political movements of the 1960s and 1970s was, unknowingly, groping for a 'new paradigm'. This framework – a kind of grand unification of new thinking – would be based, in Capra's vision, on a rejection of the mechanistic world-view inherited from Descartes and Newton, and a rediscovery of holism. All our current problems, he suggested, no matter whether they were in economics, energy supply, health care or social policy, stemmed from inappropriate understandings which were essentially of the same kind.

We live today in a globally interconnected world, in which biological, psychological, social and environmental phenomena are all interdependent. To describe the world appropriately we need an

*ecological perspective which the Cartesian world
view does not offer.*

His basic intellectual procedure was fairly simple.
Capra proposed a clear split between mechanism
and holism, and put all the ideas he discussed on
one side or the other. On the whole, he argued, bad
things stem from over-emphasis on reductionism
and mechanism, while only good can come from a
resurgence of holism. He backed this up by the
industriousness with which he compiled his
examples on both sides of the divide. Capra could
have written his book, with its long list of potential
disasters and hopeful inventory of new thinking,
without Gaia, but it fit right in with his scheme. So
it is no surprise that his chapter on the systems view
of life contains a careful, if uncritical, summary of
Lovelock and Margulis' ideas, and that the moral to
be drawn from them is clear:

*The earth, then, is a living system; it functions not
just like an organism but actually seems to be an
organism – Gaia, a living planetary being. Her
properties and activities cannot be predicted from
the sum of her parts; every one of her tissues is
linked to every other tissue and all of them are*

mutually interdependent; her many pathways of communication are highly complex and nonlinear; her form has evolved over billions of years and continues to evolve. These observations were made within a scientific context, but they go far beyond science. Like many other aspects of the new paradigm, they reflect a profound ecological awareness that is ultimately spiritual.

Small wonder that Lovelock found *The Turning Point* 'a splendid and thoughtful book' which was 'an essential guide for anyone inquiring about the place of science and metascience in our contemporary culture'.

Does this kind of thing harm the prospects of a fledgling scientific theory? Maybe not. New ideas are fair game for cultural commentators, and the worst accusation a critic could level at Capra was that his eagerness to save the world led him to exaggerate the support for some of the ideas he drew from science – as with his characterisation of the essentials of Gaia theory at the end of the 1970s as 'observations' rather than hypotheses. He may be selective, but he is accurate, and his heart is probably in the right place. He retains his fondness for Gaia in later books, such as 1996's *The Web of*

Life. But he also evinces enthusiasm there for the more recently fashionable theories of complexity and chaos, and this does not seem to have harmed their scientific standing. Perhaps his invocation of Gaia just shows how well in tune Lovelock was with what was going on in the culture.

My second example here is Rupert Sheldrake, he of morphic resonance and the book which *Nature* wanted to see burnt, and is a rather different case. Sheldrake, like Capra, has written a series of books explaining how there is more to nature, or to the Universe, than the narrow vision of established Western science can reveal. In his 1990 book *The Rebirth of Nature: The Greening of Science and God*, he devotes an entire chapter to 'The Rediscovery of Mother Earth'. In it he sees Gaia theory as part of the rise of a new animism, which regards the whole of nature as alive. This goes one better than the formulation of Gaia which just suggests that the Earth is alive. Rather, it sees that: 'The universe as a whole is a developing organism, and so are the galaxies, solar systems and biospheres within it, including the Earth.'

A few pages further on, after some diverting speculations about the 'world soul' and the Earth's magnetic and electric fields, he is happily incorporating Gaia into his own new framework for understanding development of living things. I quote here merely for flavour, so you will have to consult Sheldrake for the explanation of his novel terms:

In terms of the hypothesis of formative causation, the purposive organizing field of Gaia can be thought of as her morphic field. Such fields animate organisms at all levels of complexity, from galaxies to giraffes, and from ants to atoms. They organize, integrate and coordinate the constituent parts of organisms so that the whole system develops in accordance with its characteristic ends or goals; they maintain the integrity of the system and enable it to regenerate after damage.

Show a conventional scientist a passage like this, which strings together a whole series of huge assertions about the world without troubling us with any of the evidence which might support them, and their response will normally be along the lines: says who? Attracting advocates like this was hardly going to help Gaia's bid for scientific respectability. Indeed, young scientists were advised not to use the word, in case it jeopardised their careers. When the *New Scientist* published a couple of articles sympathetic to Gaia in the mid-1980s, the well-known microbiologist John Postgate responded with a condemnation of the idea of a planet-sized organism as 'silly and dangerous … pseudo-scientific myth-making'. It was dangerous, he argued, because it lined Gaia up alongside 'the surge of astrology, fringe medicine, faith healing, nutritional eccentricities, religious mysticism and a thousand other fads and cults which now plague developed societies'.

This invocation of all the tokens of the irrationalism which some scientists saw as threatening proper standards of inquiry shows the depths of the suspicion which use of the Earth goddess's name aroused. If the idea gained ground, Postgate asked, might not tomorrow bring 'hordes of militant Gaiaist activists enforcing some pseudoscientific idiocy on the community, crying "there is no God but Gaia and Lovelock is her prophet"?' His answer: 'All too easily.' Some of the consequences of this kind of reaction were spelled out in Lovelock's second book expanding on his ideas, which appeared in 1988.

CHAPTER IV

FROM HYPOTHESIS TO THEORY

The Ages of Gaia

Lovelock's second Gaian book was an altogether more substantial affair than the first. It was published in a series sponsored by the Commonwealth fund, edited by the doctor and writer Lewis Thomas. Thomas had produced more than one meditation on the notion of a living planet in his brilliant scientific essays, which were widely read in the 1970s, and embraced the idea of Gaia warmly as soon as he heard of it. As one of his advisors on the series was Lynn Margulis, an invitation to Lovelock to produce a new volume soon followed. It was presented as a more detailed scientific work than the first book, though still addressed to the general reader, and was a chance to give Gaia a boost after a frustrating spell when the scientific (as opposed to popular) standing of the idea seemed to be impossible to establish. 'Through the 1980s, Gaia was treated more as science fiction than as science', Lovelock recalls in his autobiography, 'and it became almost impossible to publish a paper with Gaia in the title or even in the text'. This is an exaggeration, but it is true that scientific converts were relatively few. Even those prepared to discuss the idea seriously remained sceptical. Lovelock's decade was also marked by appalling personal problems – his first wife was moving into the terminal stages of multiple sclerosis, and he himself underwent a series of painful operations after a medical mishap while recuperating from major heart surgery. He was now nearly seventy, past the age at which he would have retired from a regular job. Nevertheless, some new work and thinking got done during the decade, and the new book might give Gaia a second wind. The idea had survived enough tests, he now suggested, to be given a new status. *The Ages of Gaia* would present Gaia not as a mere hypothesis, but as a theory.

And a pretty grand theory it was. The main part of the book, as Lovelock put it, was about a new theory of evolution, 'one that does not deny Darwin's great vision but adds to it by observing that the evolution of species of organisms is not independent of the evolution of their material environment'. The book would describe the evolution of the largest organism of all – Gaia.

As befits an evolutionary narrative, the core of the book is chronological, essentially an expansion of the dozen or so pages in the earlier volume which describe the history of the Earth. It opens with a short review of the origins and history of Gaia theory, and of some of the criticisms it has met. As well as the Darwinian strictures of Doolittle and Dawkins, Lovelock highlights a critique from the earth sciences, mounted by the American climatologist Stephen Schneider, for example. Schneider's argument was that living organisms may *affect* the atmosphere, but do not *regulate* it. Other physical and chemical processes more traditionally studied by geologists are as powerful as living organisms, if not more so, and it is more accurate to think, not of homeostasis, but of co-evolution of climate and life. The organisms are not in charge, in other words. They adapt. As time goes by, they may alter environmental conditions, so have to adapt again. This two-step, extended over aeons, and over the appearance and disappearance of millions of species, accounts for the features of the modern world.

This argument, which Schneider presented in a book, *The Co-Evolution of Climate and Life*, which he co-authored in 1984, was, Lovelock now said, the more difficult one to meet, 'and in many ways the purpose of the present book is to try to answer it'. But one of his best answers, he believed, lay in one of those peculiarly modern thought experiments, a computer model, which he had devised not in response to the climate scientists, but while struggling to come up with a reply to the Darwinians. It was a toy planet which would become hotly debated in Gaian circles: Daisyworld.

Daisy, Daisy …

> *I wrestled with the problem of reducing the complexity of life and its environment to a simple scheme that could enlighten without distorting.*
>
> James Lovelock

You can study Earth systems by roaming the land and seas taking measurements – atmospheric samples, wind speeds, ocean currents, composition of rocks. Nowadays, the 'macroscopes' of orbital satellites supply vast amounts of data like this every day. You can fill out these measurements with studies of individual organisms and their internal molecular affairs. But there are two obvious limits on all of this. The Earth is immensely old, and planetary systems, especially living planets, are immensely complex. The evidence from the immediate past already tends to be poor, because most of the instruments are of recent invention. The further back you go, the thinner it gets. And the number of physical processes, chemical species, and kinds of organisms which are all interacting to produce the measured results is far too large to follow them all in detail. So a good deal of the thinking which goes into interpreting all this data is assisted by computer models.

Computer modelling basically means setting up a complex of equations to represent some variables which relate to the system you are trying to understand. Then see how they change over time as the outputs of some equations become inputs for others, through as many cycles as the silicon circuits can stand. Such models have long been important in theoretical ecology, and in environmental politics, as with the debates about the 'limits to growth' thesis that natural resources would constrain human economies in the 1970s. Today, with computers still getting faster all the time, much more complex models are argued over endlessly in the discussion of global climate change.

In the early 1980s, Lovelock was casting around for an answer to his Darwinian critics. He was especially concerned with the charge that Gaian descriptions of planetary regulation were scientifically sinful, because teleological. It was hard to write about Gaia without suggesting that the Earth organism had motives and purposes, but such ideas had long been banished from science. The Universe had no manifest destiny, in scientific terms. If it evolved, it evolved *away* from some initial state, not *towards* anything in particular. The evolution of life was an ever-branching tree, not a targeted affair. So Gaia's apparent regulation of environmental conditions did not stem from some overall imperative, a goal-seeking property of the whole system. To be allowed into the scientific mainstream, Gaian effects had to be explained non-teleologically: they had to emerge from the properties of lower-level parts of the whole, preferably ones which were compatible with natural selection.

To get a clearer view of how this might work, Lovelock came up with a thought experiment which quickly became a simple computer model, then a continuing line of research lasting for the next twenty years. The aspect of Gaia he took up was not atmosphere, awesomely complex, but temperature. Suppose, he said, there was a hypothetical planet, rather like the Earth in size and distance from a Sun-like star. Unlike the Earth, though, there is just one kind of thing growing on the planet's surface. It is a daisy, which initially comes in two varieties. In the first generation, half the daisies are dark-coloured, half light.

Now imagine that, like the Sun, this planet's star pours out more and more heat as the years go by. What would the effect be if the different-coloured daisies, as individual organisms, reflected different amounts of sunlight? Light ones bounce the star's radiation straight back. Dark ones soak it up. Both are temperature-sensitive, growing best when it is neither too hot nor too cold.

On these assumptions, the computer can plot the daisy generations and give the model planet a history. It starts off relatively cold, because the star is shining weakly. Dark daisies grow best, especially at the equator. As they trap heat, clusters of them slowly raise local temperatures so that more daisies grow. Eventually, they spread over the whole planet, which becomes warmer than it would be if a cosmic gardener dosed it with weedkiller.

Once the general ambience is warm enough, light-coloured daisies start to do better. In fact, as the star's heat output increases, there comes a point where they do better than dark ones. Local cooling, not heating, is now an advantage, and increases their reproductive success. As they come to dominate the population, the light-coloured daisies increase the whole planet's albedo – its reflectivity – and keep the global temperature in the range the flowers can tolerate. Eventually, the solar heating increases too far, and the system breaks down. Daisy populations crash and the temperature rockets. But the temperature stability of the planet model in the middle ranges of solar heat certainly looked impressive in the computer plots.

Lovelock was delighted. Now, he believed, he had an answer to the charges of teleology, of intention. The computer 'daisies' were just minding their own genetic business. But, when their behaviour was modelled using equations already well established in population biology, they produced a homeostatic effect. He called it a 'definitive rebuttal' of the suggestion that natural selection could not produce Gaian effects without some additional, goal-seeking influence in the system. Supporters of Gaia have been keen on Daisyworld ever since.

Not surprisingly, others found it less convincing. There were two main objections. One was the fairly predictable one that the properties of Lovelock's model were set up to give the results he sought, and different assumptions would give quite different results. Controversy on this score is still alive in the journals – where the current descendants of Daisyworld are very much more complicated.

The second objection was that models in themselves will persuade only those already converted. While there are models and models, this one was clearly a work of fiction. Unlike, say, global climate models, it was not tied to any real world data at all, aside from the temperature sensitivity of the flowers. There was no claim that the mechanism embodied in Daisyworld played any role in temperature regulation on Earth – where features like cloud cover would easily block its effects. Really convincing evidence for Gaia would have to come from biological, chemical and physical processes actually observed on this planet.

Still, the model was a splendid rhetorical asset, and Lovelock used it to good effect. His claims wavered a bit at times. He called it a 'parable', yet his first published paper on the model was entitled 'A cybernetic proof of the Gaia hypothesis'. At one point in his autobiography he insists that Daisyworld was never intended to be more than 'a caricature'. On the other hand:

It shows how self-regulation could be a property of a planetary system and result from the tight coupling of biological and physical evolution. Daisyworld also provides a tractable working model of the phenomenon of emergence, and is an illustration of that wonderful state when the world is more than the sum of its parts.

And he still insisted that if Daisyworld is valid, then 'seventy-five years of neo-Darwinist science will need to be rewritten'.

This kind of thing of course meant that critics attacked Daisyworld in detail as well as in principle. The first serious criticism was that a neutral-coloured Daisy could 'cheat'. Making no pigment, it would save resources, and so have an advantage over the light- or dark-coloured plants which were busy regulating the planet. Lovelock's first answer to this was to build a model in which all the daisies start grey, thus expending nothing on pigment, but have a small chance of 'mutating' into light- or dark-coloured variants. This also gave the stable behaviour shown by the simple two-daisy model. There have been many more criticisms since. Why do the daisies not adapt to temperature shifts, rather than change in ways which alter

Please Shut the Gate

Coombe Mill
Experimental
Station

Figure 9. Not a gentleman farmer but an independent theorist: Lovelock at the gate of Coombe Mill.

the temperature, for example? Lovelock's answer would be that the colour changes *are* an adaptation to the change in temperature. Many further elaborations of the models, involving more complex mathematics, have been developed along the way. A lengthy review article on 'Gaia and Natural Selection' in *Nature* in 1998 by one of Lovelock's most productive colleagues, Tim Lenton, still introduces the original two-variety Daisyworld as a basic self-regulating system. But he is quickly on to much more complex worlds, with a range of imaginary animal species. Herbivores eat daisies, and carnivores eat the herbivores. Some models have simulated food webs, featuring creatures with different preferences for different kinds of daisies. Results indicate that, some of the time at least, it is still the interaction between daisies and the environment which dominates the model, rather than, say, the appetites of the herbivores. Although the utility of such models is still not always accepted, Daisyworld, like Gaia, certainly started something.

Strong, weak and testable Gaia

Daisyworld was genuinely new, but although *Ages* was a more substantial book than *Gaia*, it did not offer much else in the way of information new to science. The novelty was more in the way Lovelock rode happily across disciplinary boundaries to tell his story of global evolution. There was a larger body of evidence presented in *Ages*, but most of it was still scavenged from the existing literature, rather than derived from Gaia-oriented research. Lovelock himself estimated that in the 1980s, 'about five' scientists, including himself and Margulis, worked on Gaia part-time. This was hardly going to transform entire disciplines, as his project demanded. At the same time, Gaia remained little discussed in regular scientific meetings. It was more likely to be debated on television as a new religion than considered as a serious scientific proposition.

This, at any rate, was the impression of the climate scientist Stephen Schneider, whom Lovelock had taken issue with in his new book. Schneider was a media-savvy senior researcher from the US National Center for Atmospheric Research already deeply involved in advocacy of policies to relieve global warming. He was interested in discussing Lovelock's ideas, though he did not necessarily agree with them. And he was in a position to do something about it.

In the late 1980s, he and two colleagues persuaded the American Geophysical Union (AGU) to devote one of its prestigious regular gatherings, the Chapman Conferences, to the Gaia hypothesis.

They had to overcome opposition in the AGU Council, and raise outside sponsorship, but the meeting was finally held in San Diego, California, in March 1988, after the main text of *Ages* was complete and a few months before publication. This conference, which brought together microbiologists and ecologists as well as more regular AGU attenders, was a landmark meeting, and the updated conference papers – which appeared three years later – the most important cross-disciplinary discussion of Gaia to date. The results, as we shall see, were mixed. But at least the idea was finally being discussed.

Lovelock himself was deeply disappointed by the meeting, which he saw in advance as 'a wonderful opportunity to establish the scientific respectability of Gaia'. This was probably unrealistic. The more radical an idea, the more stringent scientific criticism is likely to be. You can ascribe this, as Lovelock tends to, to blinkered defence of established disciplinary ways of looking at things. You can suggest, as Margulis does, that it is due to unacknowledged social and cultural influences which constrain thought. Or you can simply see it as a natural reluctance to jettison old ideas which seem to work and adopt new ones whose pay-off is uncertain. In any case, the conference was always going to produce some uncomfortable moments for the proponents of Gaia.

In the event, the most discomfort was produced by a conceptual, rather than an empirical critique. The US physicist James Kirchner offered a dissection of various versions of Gaia which its two champions had put forward over the years. There were, he suggested, no less than five separate hypotheses, starting with a weak influence of the biota on the environment, and ending up with the strongest proposal, that the biota manipulate the physical environment to create conditions optimal for life.

With hindsight, Kirchner's overall argument boils down to a fairly traditional response to the novel theory. What is true about Gaia is not new, he says, and what is new is not true. And in the printed version of his paper, it is fairly easy to pick holes in his analysis. For example, the truest version of Gaia is said to be the weakest: 'simply that the biota has a substantial influence over certain aspects of the abiotic world, such as the temperature and composition of the atmosphere'. Yet the quote from Dorion Sagan and Lynn Margulis which he used to exemplify this as one version of the Gaia hypothesis actually says: 'the temperature and composition of the Earth's atmosphere are *actively regulated* by the sum of life upon the planet' (my emphasis). This clearly means something quite different, and is a stronger and more novel thesis. The fact that Kirchner can find earlier writers – even nineteenth-century eminences like Thomas Huxley and Herbert Spencer – endorsing ideas which resemble his weakest Gaian variant then seems a less impressive demonstration of its conventionality.

At the other end of the spectrum, Kirchner belaboured some of the earliest statements about Gaia which had a teleological flavour, or even suggested that Gaia somehow 'optimises' the conditions for life. These were fair game, in one sense. Teleology was a no-go in general. And the idea of optimisation was confusing, as what was optimal for some organisms was far from attractive to others. But Lovelock's own language had since become rather more careful, so he was entitled to feel aggrieved that these earlier formulations were still targets. Rather than point this out, though, he simply got up after Kirchner's lengthy critique and asked for time to think about his comments. This seems surprising, as Kirchner had published a version of his argument in *Nature* the previous year, so it could hardly have come as a complete surprise now. But it was never Lovelock's style to confront his critics directly. Indeed, he waited until his autobiography appeared over ten years later to publicly attack Kirchner for 'sophistry'.

On the day, this presentation obviously had quite an impact. Lovelock still appears to believe that the conference was a disaster for Gaia. But the printed record tells a rather different story. The appearance in 1991 of the conference proceedings, a 400-page tome from a major university press entitled *Scientists on Gaia*, was itself a strong signal that the theory was being seriously debated. And, as well as the inevitable criticisms, the papers collected there contain numerous detailed scientific discussions of mechanisms through which Gaian effects might come about.

To take just one, G.R. Williams of the University of Toronto offered an exemplary review of what remained one of Lovelock's leading questions, and the problem with which this book began: how to explain the current level of atmospheric oxygen? As he pointed out, a Gaian explanation would win more converts if it were clear that competing explanations could not do the job. There are two aspects of the problem. First, if oxygen levels really have remained relatively constant (and not all the evidence agrees that they have), then why have they been so stable? And, even if we can explain that, why have they stayed stable at the particular level which we see today, and which seems peculiarly well suited to maximising the productivity of life once oxygen-dependent organisms have evolved? To see some possible answers, let's review the history of oxygen on Earth in a little more detail.

Recall that oxygen is a key feature of the Gaian story of terrestrial evolution. The presence of free oxygen in the atmosphere is one of the characteristics which distinguishes the Earth from Mars or Venus, and its appearance is seen as one of the most momentous events in the history of life. The evolutionary view of all this is a corrective to the human-centred view of oxygen that we tend to vaguely recall from school – in which benignly photosynthetic plants oblige us by generating the gas which we breathe. Originally, oxygen was a mere by-product, and a highly toxic one because it is so reactive, of an innovation which enabled new species of bacteria to tap a huge source of another element essential for all life, hydrogen.

Hydrogen, usually attached to carbon atoms, is

needed to manufacture the molecules that living cells are built from. But it can be hard to come by. Molecular hydrogen is very light, and tends to waft into space from the top of the atmosphere, so early life made do with hydrogen derived from hydrogen sulphide. This, too, is limited to the amounts emitted by volcanoes, but there was enough to allow simple bacteria to spread around the world. These bacteria were surrounded by a far larger store of hydrogen, but it was strongly bound to oxygen in innumerable water molecules. Hence there was advantage in evolving a machinery to trap sunlight at wavelengths energetic enough to split hydrogen from water. The first organisms to do this, probably around two billion years ago, changed the Earth forever. Within a relatively short span, geologically speaking, the concentration of atmospheric oxygen rose from one part in a million to one in five.

The result was a catastrophe for many species, for which the new environment was poisonous. But like most catastrophes, it was an opportunity for others. The opportunists eventually evolved respiration, which complements photosynthesis by making use of the oxygen. Cue a whole set of new possibilities for life, based on the eukaryotic cells (that is, ones with a nucleus and other bits of machinery that other cells lack) which Margulis made the focus of her own biological theorising. 'Before cyanobacteria split water molecules and produced oxygen', write Margulis and Sagan, 'there was no indication that earth's patina of life would ever be more than an inconspicuous scum lying on the ground.' Afterwards, life exploded into a myriad new forms, occupying many new niches.

And, somehow, the whole shebang ended up in a state where oxygen stayed high, but not too high – essentially high enough to maintain the energetically extravagant lifestyles of respirers without setting fire to them. In this Goldilocks variant of the oxygen story, Gaia acts as the engine of change, the agent of adaptation, and, ultimately, the guarantor of a new stability. As Lovelock drew the moral in his first book:

> *When oxygen leaked into the air two aeons ago, the biosphere was like the crew of a stricken submarine, needing all hands to rebuild the systems damaged or destroyed, and at the same time threatened by an increasing concentration of poisonous gases in the air. Ingenuity triumphed and the danger was overcome, not in the human way by restoring the old order, but in the flexible*

Gaian way by adapting to change and converting
a murderous intruder into a powerful friend.

It is an impressive narrative, although open to the objection that it sounds as if it makes both change *and* stability evidence for Gaian action, which is cheating. But in his paper to the San Diego conference, Williams was more interested in the stability. He acknowledged that the presence of atmospheric oxygen is due to the action of living organisms. And although data for much of the last two billion years is understandably poor, there is reasonably good evidence that atmospheric oxygen has been stable for the past 300 million years, still an impressively long span. But what actually fixes the level it reaches? That 21 per cent looks encouragingly like some kind of optimum for life, or at least some life, but could it arise by chance? Does life get what it likes, or like what it gets?

Although oxygen is generated by living organisms, since respiration appeared it is also consumed by them. In that case, the level at which the atmosphere stops accumulating oxygen will be influenced by a range of factors, which can be thought about in terms of 'sources and sinks', the traditional geochemical approach. The words can be confusing, as one sink (literally a sink in this case, as it involves dead matter drifting down to the ocean floor) is a net source of oxygen. Almost all the organic matter produced by photosynthesis is ultimately oxidised again – which takes oxygen liberated during the original photosynthesis back out of the air. But the small proportion which is hidden away in ocean floor sediments does not do this, and accounts for a modest net addition of oxygen to the atmosphere over the whole process.

Counteracting this is the oxidation of old sedimentary rocks, uplifted above the ocean over geological time, by atmospheric weathering. Volcanic gases and inorganic materials in rock like iron also take oxygen out of the air. And the rates at which all of these processes occur might be affected by the concentration of oxygen in the atmosphere, by whether sediments are deposited in deep or shallow water, by the rate of mixing of the oceans or the contours of the landscape subject to erosion, and by the supply of other chemicals, like phosphorus, which can limit the growth of living organisms.

In truth, once you try to take account of all the many factors which can be invoked as influences on oxygen depletion and release, and the even larger number of ways in which they interact, it is quite possible to come up with models in which ordinary chemical and geological processes determine the outcome, without any biologically-mediated feedbacks. As the details of all these processes are complex, and imperfectly understood, it is easy to believe that, in principle, they can solve the problem.

Thus Williams begins by detailing some of these non-Gaian explanations for levels of atmospheric oxygen. There are geochemical explanations, involving reaction between oxygen and minerals in rocks and soil. There are geophysical explanations, in which feedbacks between the rate of deposition of organic material in the ocean and the level of oxygen in seawater are influenced by volume and rate of circulation of the oceans. And there are biogeochemical explanations, such as influences on living growth – mainly of tiny phytoplankton – of the amount of phosphate in the ocean.

Only then does he discuss a fully Gaian explanation, in which biological effects somehow select 20 per cent of atmospheric oxygen as optimal for the new classes of aerobic (oxygen-using) organisms. This he eventually rejects, on the grounds that the 'optimal' level for some organisms would have to be maintained by others which do not benefit from it. Here he echoes Kirchner in suggesting that some versions of the Gaia hypothesis are too strong to pass serious scrutiny, although unlike Kirchner he acknowledges that Lovelock stopped explicitly claiming the optimising tendency of Gaia in the early 1980s.

However, along the way Williams also makes a more subtle argument. By going through the details of the various possible mechanisms, he shows how biological processes are involved in various ways even when the main drivers are chemical or physical. Once life is ubiquitous, it gets involved in chemical cycling for its own purposes. For example, if the oxygen affinities of crucial enzymes in marine organisms were altered, a different balance would be struck between the rates at which oxygen disappears into rocks and is generated in the oceans. Or if the properties of enzymes which actively transport phosphate across cell membranes of ocean-living phytoplankton shift, this would affect the ocean biogeochemistry of oxygen significantly.

As the complexities of all these interacting sources and sinks – and the routes between them – unfold, one reading is that there is almost bound to be biological involvement. It is simply a matter of degree. In that case, Gaia theory is less radical than it has been made out to be. That, perhaps, makes it more acceptable. And Williams also suggests that there are Gaian aspects to the ostensibly simpler geochemical or geophysical explanations. What remains harder to tease out is whether there are not just links between all these processes – physical, chemical and biological – but also feedback loops in which the biological parts of the system control some critical path. It is closure of these loops which needs to be demonstrated if Gaia theory is to carry real conviction as a regulatory framework.

As I've said, Williams' own conclusion in 1991 was that Gaia as homeostasis *by* the biosphere was relatively uncontroversial in this case, but that homeostasis *for* the biosphere was harder to support because it would not just require present-day chemical and biochemical feedbacks. There would have to be a line of reasoning which would show why marine micro-organisms would evolve in ways which benefit land-based oxygen breathers. This sounds like the old Darwinist objection again, and it is. But making it so specific makes it easier to go and look for evidence which might counter it. At this point, there is at least the possibility of an argument which moves beyond the exchange of review papers and begins to develop into a research programme. This was not much comfort to Lovelock, who was heading into old age and had been trying to promote his ideas for twenty years. But here, as elsewhere in the conference proceedings, there are important glimpses of what such a research programme might look like. Some undoubtedly left San Diego encouraged to think of mechanisms and measurements which would help unravel the precise details of the cycles of oxygen and of other key elements. Not a bad result from a meeting which could easily have turned out to be a serious setback for Gaia, but in fact did not.

· CHAPTER V ·

FROM GAIA TO GEOPHYSIOLOGY

Mulling over metaphors

> [E]*very metaphor is the tip of a submerged model …*
>
> Max Black

Part of the reason for Lovelock's frustration with his fellow scientists in San Diego was that he had moved further on from his initial formulations of Gaia than most of them seemed to realise. This was true in several ways. He had, as *The Ages of Gaia* made clear, worked harder to eliminate teleological overtones, and suggestions that the living Earth had intentions. But he had also become clearer about what kind of hypothesis, or now theory, Gaia was. Perhaps if *Ages* had appeared before the conference, the meeting might have treated him more kindly. Earlier on, as the book *Gaia* showed, he was dealing with ideas at a host of different levels – as newly-formulated scientific notions tend to –

and happily mixing them up. One minute he was the trained scientist, discussing redox potentials and chemical equilibria. The next he was speaking with the voice of the prophet, speculating about whether the advent of *Homo sapiens* confers consciousness on Gaia. In the decade of environmental awareness, of Spaceship Earth, and suggestions that science was the standard-bearer for mechanism, materialism, reductionism and other undesirable 'isms' which obscured more enlightened ways of seeing, there was a strong temptation to become a guru of a holistic, interactive, cybernetic, democratic way of thinking. Its watchwords would be emergence and co-operation. It would be rooted in science but moving beyond it into questions about the meaning of life and right conduct on the planet. It was not a temptation that Lovelock was able to resist, although, independent-minded as ever, he was as much a critic as a friend to the environmental movement. Even in *Ages*, he devoted chapters to Gaia and the contemporary environment, and to God and Gaia.

As I suggested when discussing Capra and Sheldrake, the more Gaia appealed to 'New Age' movements, the less attractive it seemed to mainstream science. But while this mixture of messages made it harder for other scientists to engage with Lovelock's ideas, they needed a better reason to disregard the specifics of Gaia than that it kept company with other ideas they did not care for. One charge was simply that Gaia was not a serious scientific hypothesis as it was merely a metaphor, not a set of testable propositions. The whole point about metaphors, James Kirchner wrote, was that they are not supposed to be literally true: 'Treating a metaphor as a scientific proposition that is factually true or false is simply a waste of time.'

It was quite easy to argue that this was much too restrictive a view of the role of metaphors in development of scientific ideas. At its simplest, a metaphor is a statement that one thing is 'like' another, and it draws attention to some features of both the things in question at the expense of others. New scientific metaphors often join something known with something whose properties are as yet undefined, so are an invitation to go and look for the features that the metaphor seems to imply. When metaphors are used in science, and they are often indispensable, they are eventually evaluated on whether the likenesses they suggest prompt further thoughts about more detailed similarities, more specific hypotheses which fit the overall framework. Indeed, a very similar point was made at the Chapman Conference by John Kineman of the US National Oceanic and Atmospheric Administration:

The value of theory ... cannot be judged on the testability of its assumptions and definitions, but rather on its performance as a structure for scientific thought. It is, in contrast, individual processes or mechanisms proposed within theory that can be tested empirically. This distinction between assumptions and causal processes of theory is critical to evaluating new concepts such as strong Gaia.

There were other possible responses. Darwin's natural selection itself began as a metaphor, comparing what happens in nature with the unnatural selection practised by animal breeders, but that did not stop it generating a rather fruitful branch of scientific theory. And critics of Gaia themselves made unacknowledged assumptions. In particular, the metaphorical roots of mechanistic science in the clockwork universe which Newton placed at the heart of Western thought were still constraining ideas, some advocates of Gaia suggested.

There was doubtless some truth in this, but there were also some confusions which were little remarked on at the time. This was mainly because Lovelock usually found it convenient to fall in with the assumption of writers like Capra that there is a straightforward opposition between 'organic' and 'mechanical' – or holist versus reductionist – world-views. The idea of Earth as a living organism was then identified with the organic, holistic tradition. Yet this is too simple a view. On one hand, if Earth is an organism, that need not mean that it cannot operate mechanistically, as the Cartesian tradition of the body-machine would have it. On the other, conceptions of machinery have become much more complex than the clockwork envisaged by the Newtonians. The explicitly acknowledged origin of an important set of Gaian ideas lies in a more sophisticated view of machines, which in turn has given rise to general theories of systems and control. Modern ideas about cybernetics are as applicable to organisms as to machines, and indeed Lovelock tends to switch between the two when he is explaining them. As soon as the steam engine – a classic example, and one which Lovelock uses – acquired a governor which opened valves according to its speed of rotation, it had a self-regulating device built into it. But once you know what to look for, the living world is full of examples of similar devices.

Gaia, then, can be seen not as an attempt to revive an organic world-view at the expense of a mechanical one, but as the product of the continuing exchange between them. It could even just be part of a general trend for two of our great governing metaphors to converge – as organisms become machine-like, so machines become more like living creatures. Either way, the fact that Gaia theory trades in metaphors need not itself be a problem for its use as a basis for further scientific exploration. What was still a problem, of course, was that William Golding's name for the original hypothesis, however beguiling, carried a host of additional meanings with it. An invitation to venerate Mother Earth is simply an embarrassment in a scientific context. Scientists may be happy to use metaphors, but they prefer ones which do not have quite such a complex train of associations, or ones whose baggage, at any rate, is less visible. Lovelock, for his part, eventually wanted to contribute to a discussion in which the premise was not necessarily that the Earth is alive, but that some aspects of the Earth's systems bear comparison with a giant organism. That would afford scope for the discussion to turn into a research programme investigating exactly which aspects of Earth work this way.

One way out of the identification of Earth as organism was signalled by Margulis. She was never very happy with the idea of the planet as a single living entity, and offered a range of other ways of describing Gaia as a biological system, mainly drawing on ecological imagery. As she put it in her book *The Symbiotic Planet* (1998), 'Gaia itself is not an organism directly selected among many. It is an emergent property of interaction among organisms, the spherical planet on which they reside, and an energy source, the sun.' Or, a little later: 'Gaia is the series of interacting ecosystems that compose a single huge ecosystem at the Earth's surface. Period.'

With that in mind, and recognising that Gaia had become as much of a liability as an asset, Lovelock proposed a different shift in the core metaphor. If the various disciplines which might have something to say about the Earth were to come together – from chemistry to geochemistry to biogeochemistry – they should do so, he suggested, under the banner of geophysiology.

Planetary medicine – who's the doctor?

The shift was in some ways a small one. The idea that study of the Earth was like investigating regulation of a complex organism was already laid out in Lovelock's first book, with its invocation of homeostasis. But the coinage of geophysiology came later, in a 1986 paper in the *Bulletin* of the American Meteorological Society. By the time *Ages* appeared, it was a central part of the introductory pitch. With characteristically charged rhetoric, Lovelock asked why the Earth and life sciences have 'been torn apart by the ruthless dissection of science into separate but blinkered disciplines'? It was time for Gaia theory to be the basis of a new and unified view of the Earth and life sciences. And, 'because Gaia was seen from outside as a physiological system, I have called the science of Gaia geophysiology'.

This was cleverly ambiguous. Was Gaia as a larger idea not science, then, but something separate from it? Perhaps not. Or perhaps scientists who wanted to pursue Lovelock's ideas could use a proper, scientific-sounding name instead of the flaky one they had first heard. If so, he was willing to go along. At a meeting in Oxford in the mid-1990s, he even suggested abandoning Gaia altogether in favour of geophysiology, but activists such as the environmentalist Jonathon Porritt and the radical geneticist Mae-Wan Ho argued strongly against this bit of linguistic self-denial. They felt that the inspiration of Gaia for non-scientists was too important to lose.

Even so, geophysiology was a fertile metaphor to explore, and in *Ages* Lovelock began to develop the associated notion of 'planetary medicine'. This would of necessity be practised in the same way as normal medicine had been until around the middle of the twentieth century: able to diagnose disease but without any real idea what to do about most of it. Nevertheless, it was a useful conceit for describing some contemporary environmental problems like global warming, acid rain, ozone depletion or nuclear radiation. It was one he shortly expanded to book length in a volume variously titled *The Practical Science of Planetary Medicine* (in the UK) or *Healing Gaia* (in the US), in which he restated much of the material in *Ages*, using more explicitly medical terminology. But he began with a more formal statement of what his point of view implied, making it clear that homeostasis was still the heart of the matter:

> [T]o a geophysiologist, a living organism is a
> bounded system open to a flux of matter and
> energy, which is able to keep its internal medium
> constant in composition, and its physical state
> intact in a changing environment; it is able to keep
> in **homeostasis**. This geophysiologist's definition
> of life includes Gaia. The Earth is bounded on the
> outside by space with which it exchanges energy,
> sunlight coming in and heat radiation going out. It
> is bounded on the inside by inner space, the vast
> volume of plastic hot rock that supports the crust
> and with which the crust exchanges matter. It is
> reasonable to consider the Earth as a system in
> homeostasis.

In both books, the physiological-cum-medical
metaphor enabled Lovelock to elaborate his position on contemporary environmentalism, shorn of
the associations of Earth-worship evoked by Gaia.
Thus, the contemporary world is found to be suffering from carbon dioxide fever, acid indigestion,
ozonemia. All are potentially serious, though
rising carbon dioxide is the most worrying. On a
different topic, which preoccupied environmental
campaigners, Lovelock in his role as self-appointed
planetary physician saw nuclear radiation as

something life can cope with. Like oxygen, it presents opportunities as well as threats.

On a global scale, though, the greatest harm is caused by bad farming, with large-scale changes in land use adding to the problems of carbon dioxide release. Here, as in other cases, Lovelock's concern is to shift the questions asked, and consider how stable the earth system is, and what scales of perturbation it can cope with. And while evoking a strong environmental concern, he also stresses that Gaia as a whole is unlikely to be threatened by any changes brought about by humans. The problem is more that we might provoke a shift to a new stable state which would be much less to our own liking than the one we have benefited from for the last thousands of years. For now, as he put it in *Healing Gaia*, the planet is suffering from *Disseminated Primatemia*, a plague of people. As with many of his throwaway remarks, this was ambiguous, suggesting that he aligned with those, usually in the wealthy countries, complaining about 'overpopulation'. Perhaps he would have done better to stick with his oft-used summary of the three worst human-induced threats to planetary stability: 'cars, cattle and chainsaws'.

The geophysiological idea was also a fruitful way for others to approach Gaia, as New York University biologist Tyler Volk did with a slight twist to the metaphor in his book *Gaia's Body: Towards a Physiology of the Earth*, a notable popularisation of work on biogeochemical cycles. In describing such systems, the more conventional idea of geochemical cycles – in which key elements move between ocean, air or rock reservoirs through chemical action – is modified through incorporating biological influences on the reactions which occur. The key question is then whether the biologically catalysed reactions determine the overall rates of circulation.

For Volk, there was inspiration in Gaian ideas to look for biological involvement almost no matter where the chemistry under study was taking place. Lovelock had already revisited the macrocosm–microcosm analogy in his discussion of geophysiology in *Healing Gaia*:

> *With living organisms the intensity of life varies from part to part. Your hair, your nails and the outer layers of your teeth contain no living cells, yet they are undeniably a part of you. So it is with the atmosphere, the oceans and the crustal rocks of the Earth: they are parts of the organism in which life is thinly dispersed.*

Volk went into even more detail. In the latter part of his book he argued for Gaian effects at the level of a small number of physiologically important molecules which are found in a great many species. Following work by the American biochemist G.J. Williams, he suggested that the detailed molecular properties of a few key enzymes lead to fine-tuning of planetary-scale chemical cycles. As with regular physiology, in other words, study of Gaia is enhanced by the, to some, old-fashioned reductionism of molecular biology. Volk's book was an impressive demonstration that there were new links to make between Gaian ideas and more established science. In that way, it was a sign of how things were starting to move Lovelock's – or Gaia's – way. But the Gaia which would emerge as an influence on large-scale science over the next decade or so would be a tamer, more carefully house-trained beast than the living Earth goddess who had been introduced to her human subjects back in the 1970s.

CHAPTER VI

FROM GEOPHYSIOLOGY TO EARTH SYSTEM SCIENCE

Short of a Nobel Prize, it can be hard to say when a new idea becomes scientifically legitimate. With something as complex as the Earth, and theories of global interaction, there was never likely to be a crucial prediction or a vital experiment which could be used to lever opinion. Rather, the approach suggested by the Gaia hypothesis has gradually gained ground through the efforts of a relatively small band of scientists who pursued one aspect or another of the regulation of atmosphere and climate. Many researchers in those fields stuck to conventional approaches, but enough incorporated biological systems in their thinking, and empha-sised the importance of control and feedback, to begin to make a difference. By drawing other scientists into arguments about the details, rather than the grand hypothesis, they made the whole enterprise look more like conventional science.

This happened in a number of areas, but perhaps most impressive is the new view of the global sulphur cycle and how it may be linked to climate. It is not just a good illustration of a new, multi-disciplinary approach to biospheric interactions. It may even be the area where some of the fundamental, Darwinian, objections to strong Gaia can be at least partially met.

Sulphur and sunshades

Go back to one of the first discoveries which derived from Gaian ideas, the production of dimethyl sulphide (DMS) in the oceans. As we saw earlier, Lovelock reasoned that there should be an atmospheric carrier gas which helped complete the geo-chemical sulphur cycle by transferring the element from sea to land. He believed that DMS was a promising candidate. And when he went to sea, continual monitoring revealed that DMS was present pretty much as he predicted, if not always in quite the right amounts.

Here was just what was needed to inspire further research: a new empirical finding which raised as many questions as answers. Since that first report of DMS thirty years ago, work on exactly where the gas comes from, and on what its effects might be, has become the best example of a Gaian-inspired research programme. Interpretations of the results include some of the strongest claims to have identified real feedback loops between chemical reactions happening inside living tissue and possible effects on global climate. The DMS story has also produced some tantalising suggestions about how such feedbacks could evolve through normal natural selection operating on micro-organisms living in the sea. In addition, it offers intriguing illustrations of the unpredicted twists and turns, and unexpected ideas, which inevitably punctuate fruitful research. Let's look in more detail at some of these ideas as a case study in how Gaian thinking can develop.

The first idea was simply that there ought to be some gaseous sulphur carrier, and that living things in the ocean might supply it. It seemed at least plausible that they were doing so, in amounts large enough to account for the difference between the quantities of sulphur actually being produced on land and the amount being flushed into the sea. Three further big questions governed the research which followed. Why did the micro-organisms bother to make DMS? Did it have any other influences on the environment aside from simple sulphur transport? And was there any way to link those effects to benefits to the organisms doing the first bit of chemistry? Most importantly, was there a chain of cause and effect which might give them a selective advantage?

By the time *Ages* was written, there were tentative answers to the first question, at least. One seemed to be that microscopic organisms in the oceans do not make DMS directly, but do make a more complex compound called dimethylsulphonio-propionate. This is one of a class of compounds called betaines (after similar chemicals first found in beets) which have an unusual structure, with separated positive and negative charges in different parts of the same molecule. Their advantage for marine organisms is that they offer some protection against the osmotic stresses produced by high concentrations of salt.

Why do they need protecting? Osmosis is a physical effect which arises when there is a division between two solutions with unequal concentrations. If the two solutions are mixed, the concentration of the dissolved substance – say sugar or salt in water – tends to even out, in the same way that mixing hot and cold fluids tends to produce a lukewarm result. Now imagine that the two fluid reservoirs are the cell of an ocean-dwelling organism and the effectively infinite sea surrounding it. The salt concentration inside the cell is typically less than one third that of the sea-water. And the cell, to carry on the business of living at all, has to maintain a barrier which defines its inside and outside, but which allows a range of atoms, ions and molecules in and out. Problem: the osmotic pressure wants to even out the salt concentrations on both sides of the barrier, the cell membrane. As the volumes are so different, the water inside the cell can make no difference to the salinity of the ocean. So the cell has to have mechanisms for regulating what passes across the membrane. These fight the continual tendency for salt to enter the cell as sodium and chloride ions, and for water to leave. Giving in to either would be fatal.

Obviously, cells can manage this, and the details are fascinating but need not detain us here. Imagine lots of tiny molecular machines continually running uphill. But this all needs energy, and sometimes emergency back-up. This is where betaines could be useful. Their separated positive and negative charges can neutralise a certain amount of chloride and sodium ions, and so protect the internal environment of the cell should the salt content increase. Perhaps they first evolved, Lovelock suggested, in organisms which live inshore and are prone to getting stranded in pools of evaporating seawater. Without betaines, osmosis would increase the salt concentration inside the organism – they are usually species of marine algae – far enough to kill them. With betaines, they can tolerate the increased salt.

So much for the benefit to individual, evolving organisms at the first stage in the process. But what might all this have to do with Gaia? To be involved in global regulation of sulphur transfer, there had to be a plausible story linking betaines to processes taking longer than evaporation from pools of seawater, and operating over longer distances. To begin with, Lovelock's speculations were limited to a kind of reciprocal fertilisation.

The scenario went like this. When betaine-synthesising algae eventually die off, the compound breaks down and releases DMS as a by-product. This might waft inshore where it would eventually decompose in its turn, and increase availability of sulphur on land. As some land plants find sulphur scarce, this would increase their growth. Here, Lovelock invoked an important result already reasonably well established by Gaian-inspired research – that the presence of living organisms can increase the rate of weathering of rocks. This has led to another continuing line of research investigating how enhanced weathering affects atmospheric composition. But its relevance here was simply that it might increase nutrient run-off from land into the ocean. Lovelock's first formulation then concluded with what, with hindsight, reads like a characteristic bit of hand-waving:

It is not difficult to explain the mutual extension of the land-based ecosystems from the supply of sulphur and of the sea-based ecosystems from the increased flux of nutrients. But through this, or some similar series of small steps, the intricate geophysiological regulation systems evolve.

Well, perhaps. But the devil would be in the detail, which would depend on more research, leading to estimates of how much of what chemicals were actually being transported in each direction, and how fast. And the numbers generated would have to convince scientists who were looking for tight arguments, not just plausible stories.

Still, that might have been enough to stimulate further research on the larger role of DMS. But there quickly arose a more startling idea. Perhaps the gas was involved, not just in sulphur cycling, and hence global chemical equilibrium, but in the other major Gaian sphere of operations: climate.

Now the key notion was not fertilisation of land plants but something more lofty – cloud seeding. Once in the air, DMS oxidises to produce sulphur dioxide, and then sulphuric acid. Small droplets of sulphuric acid are excellent nuclei for condensation of water vapour, and hence cloud formation. If DMS is not just produced by inshore organisms, but is also generated by creatures which live in the open seas, more DMS from marine organisms could mean more clouds over the ocean. Since oceans are dark and clouds are light, more DMS might also mean more solar radiation reflected back into space. Here, perhaps, was a link between some of the smallest organisms in the sea and global temperature control.

There was already evidence that big volcanic eruptions reduce global temperatures because they leave a fine suspension of sulphuric acid particles in the stratosphere. Perhaps oceanic organisms might do something similar at lower altitude. Hypothetically, an increase in temperature might boost growth of marine algae, raise DMS levels, and hence cloud cover. This in turn would increase the

Earth's ability to reflect solar radiation, its albedo, and reduce the temperature again.

Once again, the possible feedback had been described. But it raised a whole set of further questions. How much DMS would you need to have an appreciable effect? Did sulphur dioxide at low altitudes produce cloud droplets of the right size? Was there any evidence that cloud cover over the oceans fluctuated under the influence of such factors? And, always in the background, the larger Darwinian question. Why would it be in the interests of minute oceanic organisms to contribute to the maintenance of a planetary sunshade?

A host of new investigations followed. Some of these were simply extensions of existing work on the intricacies of global sulphur fluxes. A recent textbook lists 17 different chemical and physical transformations of sulphur in the atmosphere alone, of which over half are multi-step processes. As sulphur tends to stay in the atmosphere for days rather than weeks or years, there can be big local variations in the concentration of individual sulphur compounds high in the air, depending on what is happening down below. Small wonder, then, that estimates of the annual amounts of any individual sulphur compound passing through the atmosphere often vary considerably. Best guesses for annual global production of sulphur-containing gases in the ocean – mainly DMS – have come down by a factor of three since the early 1970s, for example.

In addition to sharpening up figures like this, there were efforts to work out the biochemistry of more marine organisms, many of which are little-studied, in more detail. Atmospheric chemists refined their understanding of what happens to DMS when it encounters the complex mix of gases in the air. Ice cores from the Antarctic were analysed to see how much sulphur they contained, and in what form. Meteorologists became more interested in wind speed over the oceans, in how long clouds persist, and in the microphysics of cloud formation. Added together, it was just the kind of multi-disciplinary inquiry Lovelock had always advocated.

The results did not always make the picture clearer, nor get closer to cracking the evolutionary problem. The regulation of the production of DMS, via betaines, and its ultimate fate, was not straight-forward. In some organisms there was evidence that the by-products of betaines were a defence mechanism against viruses (the sea is full of them), a possible addition to their osmotic advantages.

It became apparent that understanding sulphur cycling would also require teasing out details of the geophysiology of iodine – another important trace element, and one which speeds up some of the reactions governing the fate of atmospheric sulphur. And selective advantages for the putative large-scale effects of DMS production remained largely speculative. Perhaps the fact that increased cloud cover tends to increase wind-speed over the oceans helped mix surface waters and supply more nutrients to the algae. But how would that link to global temperature? Besides, if betaine production was affected by salinity, then the increase in salt content of the seas through additional freezing near the poles as temperature decreased, and thickening ice-caps, could even generate a positive feedback. Maybe marine organisms were partly responsible for ice ages?

Still, some in the field became more convinced that something close to the originally proposed Gaian mechanism was at work. Lovelock's British colleagues Andrew Watson and Peter Liss of the University of East Anglia went so far as to name a figure for the global cooling effect of present-day marine organisms. In a review published in the *Philosophical Transactions of the Royal Society* in

1998, they suggested that on average the world is 6 degrees cooler than it would be without the action of ocean life, and that two thirds of this decrease is due to DMS. But they still acknowledged that the climate feedback produced by DMS was as likely to be positive, and hence lead to instability, as negative. And the link with an individual organism's reproductive fitness was still the slightly tenuous one of enhanced nutrient supply produced by cloud-dependent winds stirring up the ocean, or carrying mineral-rich dust from land far out to sea. There was a variant hypothesis that heating the sea surface induced stratification of ocean waters, with a relatively stable warm layer sitting above the cold depths, and that this restricted algal growth lower down. But neither carried great conviction. To really make people sit up, there had to be another new idea.

A *really* extended phenotype

The next suggestion for explaining why algae seem to help regulate the climate came from one of the sharpest practitioners of evolutionary theory, the late Bill Hamilton of Oxford University. Hamilton was a man of wide-ranging scientific interests (he died in 2001 from an illness contracted on an African field trip investigating AIDS), but his main claim to fame was his contribution to the theory of inclusive fitness. This was the idea that an individual organism would only behave in a way which benefited another if there was a reasonable chance that they both had genes in common. It was essentially the same idea as Richard Dawkins' 'selfish gene', and Dawkins was the first to acknowledge Hamilton as one of his main influences. He was thus a Darwinian of impeccable credentials, and his most important work fed directly into the strong criticisms of Gaia from fellow devotees of gene selection. But in the 1990s, he became intrigued by the Gaian discussions around DMS, and talked them over with Tim Lenton, a young researcher who had studied with Lovelock and was now carving out his own scientific career. Hamilton accepted that small ocean organisms were making the stuff in large quantities. What might be the reason from their point of view?

His answer was that they could have a fundamental biological interest at stake: not reproduction but dispersal. It was well recognised in evolutionary theory that a species which could find a new way of getting from place to place increased its chances of survival. And there was increasing evidence that micro-organisms can travel inter-continental distances through the air. If you are small enough, once you are airborne you can stay there and just move with the wind. Still, where did DMS come in? There did not seem to be a problem with a few individual algae making the leap from sea to air. A few bursting bubbles in oceanic foam would take care of that. But Hamilton and Lenton reckoned that DMS could help some algal species reach the higher altitudes needed to take advantage of the winds to cover really long distances.

It would work like this. An algal bloom, with its trillions of individual organisms, would release a significant concentration of DMS into the air directly above. As this turns into sulphur dioxide it makes tiny water droplets condense, releasing heat and warming the air. Warm air rises, and the fortunate algae ride the updraft. The main snag was that oxidation of DMS is normally so slow that the algae would drift away before the air warmed up. But some observations from the early 1990s suggested that it could all happen much faster. Once again, there were plenty of details to be worked out, but it really looked as if at least one potential Gaian loop could have evolved through selective advantage for the organisms involved. Hamilton was impressed enough with the whole approach to support Lovelock and Gaia more emphatically than any other prominent evolutionist. He went so far as to compare Lovelock to Copernicus – like the astronomer who suggested that the Earth moves round the Sun, he had a big idea which others found hard to accept, and was waiting for his Newton to explain how it could all work.

It is traditional for supporters of heterodox scientific theories to invoke Galileo, on the logically dubious grounds that because one novel idea which we believe is correct was resisted, that makes another idea which meets resistance more likely to be true. The Copernican analogy is a little more sophisticated. And Hamilton is not the only observer of Gaian developments to invoke Copernicus. The German climate scientist H.J. Schellnhuber has proposed that the whole notion of Earth system science (on which more below) will culminate in a second Copernican-style revolution, permanently altering our view of the planet.

So far as Lovelock's formulation of Gaia goes, however, the comparison with Copernicus is a good compliment but a bad analogy. True, the

Copernican revolution entailed a drastic shift in world-view, and Lovelock was advocating a new way of looking at things. But Copernicus' theory was strictly an either/or proposition. If he was right, the Sun was at the centre of the Universe, or at least the Solar System. If not, the older, Earth-centred view could remain undisturbed. But the Gaian proposition was more complex, richly associative, and open to modification in ways which made it less radical than it first seemed. There can be effects without feedback, feedbacks without optimisation, maintenance of stability without the Earth acting in the fully integrated fashion of a living organism. Even so, Hamilton's comment was a big change from the initial indifference or hostility which greeted Gaia among scientists. Lovelock's ideas were starting to inspire some serious, novel scientific thinking.

And the DMS story is only one of the tales which could be told to show how thoughts inspired by the original Gaia hypothesis have led to a whole trail of research and ideas which have yielded new insights into interactions between life and environment with large-scale effects. Some are much more recent. For example, in 2002, it was reported in *Nature* that organic iodide vapours emitted by marine algae are oxidised in the air to produce a hitherto unrecognised source of aerosol particles. Just like sulphur dioxide, these can affect atmospheric temperatures both by their own scattering effects on incoming solar radiation, and by acting as cloud condensation nuclei. At the moment, this conclusion is based on a mixture of local observations in the Irish Sea, laboratory experiments on simulated atmospheric smogs, and modelling of what might happen if the findings were scaled up to the planetary level. But the kind of research which has been done on the DMS system shows what kind of measurements to make in the wide ocean to see if this new geobiochemical path can generate climatic effects. This, too, is how research programmes become truly productive: not by radical advances, but by moving into closely related but distinct areas where what has already been done suggests what to do next.

· CHAPTER VII ·

GAIA GETS RESPECTABLE

Work like the studies of sulphur and iodine certainly helped Gaia gain a foothold in more conservative scientific circles. However, there were more general developments in science, and support for science, which made the world a more hospitable place for at least some aspects of the Gaian approach. These stemmed partly from the need to discover more about global systems in order to understand how they might cope – or fail to cope – with changes induced by the things that billions of people were doing.

It seems fair to label the unexpected mechanisms which rely on DMS or iodine compounds 'geo-physiology'. But the term which is more often heard today to cover all these studies, and more, is 'Earth system science'. Like geophysiology, this is less evocative than Gaia, but its influence makes up for what it loses in terms of poetry. And on examination it signifies the ascendancy of a new approach to planetary studies which owes a good deal to the multi-disciplinary mantra of Lovelock and his supporters. The name was first publicised in a report from NASA in 1986, but has since become much more widely accepted. Moves to establish this approach have arisen in large part because of efforts to understand the short-term global changes which have become a major concern of environmentalists over the last thirty years – especially atmospheric change and global warming. A succession of international research programmes have reflected the growing political urgency of global environmental issues, notably the International Geosphere-Biosphere Programme and the World Climate Research Programme. Getting a clearer idea of the effects which human activity may have on climate, for example, requires a much more detailed understanding of how the global system worked in the absence of all the carbon dioxide and sulphur which industry now pours into the atmosphere. That, in turn, entails just the kind of inquiry into the interactions between atmosphere, oceans, rocks, and living organisms which investigation of Gaia also implies.

This does not mean that Earth system science is synonymous with Gaia, or vice-versa. It is an umbrella term for a vast range of inquiries into distinct aspects of the Earth. But its guiding principle is that as well as breaking them into their constituent parts, the various Earth systems must be understood in their interactions, must somehow be re-integrated. And this turns out to be a way of expressing the tension between reductionism and holism which enables more and more scientists to locate their work in a larger framework. It is also a label which funding agencies are happy to attach to programmes and institutes, which always helps.

The extent to which current work on global change and Earth systems is imbued with the ideas promoted by Lovelock, at least programmatically, was shown by a statement drawn up for a joint meeting of some of the most important current research programmes held in Amsterdam in July 2001, and endorsed by over 1,000 delegates. The Amsterdam Declaration on Global Change tried to express the views of the scientific communities of four international global change research pro-grammes – the International Geosphere-Biosphere Programme (IGBP), the International Human Dimensions Programme on Global Environmental Change (IHDP), the World Climate Research Pro-gramme (WCRP) and the international biodiversity programme DIVERSITAS. Although the emphasis of all four is on understanding the causes and consequences of global change induced by human activity, the larger scientific picture is important too. So the second paragraph of the statement suggests that:

Research carried out over the past decade under the auspices of the four programmes to address these concerns has shown that:

> *The Earth System behaves as a single, self-regulating system comprised of physical, chemical, biological and human components. The interactions and feedbacks between the component parts are complex and exhibit multi-scale temporal and spatial variability. The understanding of the natural dynamics of the Earth System has advanced greatly in recent years and provides a sound basis for evaluating the effects and consequences of human-driven change.*

This is some way from being a Gaian manifesto, and it certainly does not say that the Earth is alive. But the embrace of 'self-regulation', however complex, is also a long way from the mind-set of the Earth sciences in the early 1960s. The wording also appears to confirm the verdict of Lee Kump of Penn State University in the USA, a long-time observer of the Gaian discussion, that a major effect of Lovelock's thinking has been to shift attention away from the pools of Earth's major elements and the movements between them, and towards identifying control systems and feedbacks. Of course, this might have happened without Gaia, but it is hard to argue that the theory did not help it along.

For all that, how Gaian Earth systems science turns out to be will depend on a great deal of future research. But it already seems to bear the imprint of Gaia, in general if not always in detail. One test of success for a scientific theory is appearance in the textbooks, and here Gaia is certainly gaining ground. In the mid-1990s, it was still possible for Brian Skinner and Stephen Porter, of Yale and the University of Washington respectively, to produce a complete college textbook on Earth system science without a mention of Lovelock or Gaia. But they are beginning to look a little behind the times. In 1992, a similar multi-author textbook on *Global Biogeochemical Cycles* was already giving Gaia a little house-room, though it was still confined to passing mentions. The first chapter cites Gaia as a 'novel hypothesis', while the last mentions Lovelock's use of geophysiology as a term for multi-disciplinary investigation of the whole Earth.

Eight years later, though, the second edition of the same book was retitled *Earth System Science*, and presents the advent of Gaia as a major transition to a way of seeing that 'the biosphere is ultimately what ties the major systems of the Earth together'. The whole text is framed by a 'philosophy of integration' which states that it is necessary not only to study all the geospheres (air, water, rocks and soil) and all of the biogeochemical cycles (carbon, nitrogen, sulphur, phosphorus and trace metals), but to bring them all together. 'The functioning of the biosphere and each of the individual physical spheres of the planet involves continuous and strong interactions, making all parts of the earth system dependent to some degree on all the other parts.' As is the way with textbooks, there is then a name-check for revered ancestors, and the reader is informed that: 'disciplinary science has provided little in the way of precedent for us, although substantial guidance is provided by the pioneers like Arrhenius, Vernadsky and Lovelock who presaged these global developments'.

Judging the influence of Lovelock's ideas thereafter is a matter of reading between the lines. The form of the Gaia hypothesis which is eventually presented is relatively weak: 'the modified form of Gaia postulates only that the activities of living organisms have had, and continue to have, major effects on the composition of the atmosphere. It does not specify why organisms have evolved those features.' But although Gaia is not a major plank of the book, it is replete with detailed analyses of the chemistry, biology and physics of planetary cycles which bear the stamp of Gaian thinking. Even the range of disciplines brought together is significant. The 28 individual authors work in departments or institutes of atmospheric sciences, engineering, geology, astronomy, geography, oceanography, meteorology, radiochemistry, zoology, microbiology, plant science and forestry. The book consistently emphasises that the precise couplings between all the systems they outline, and the size of their effects, usually remain uncertain, and that there are many poorly understood factors to take into account. On the role of particles in the atmosphere, which is such a central part of the DMS story I have related at length, for example, the authors simply say that 'their role in climate poses an almost entirely open set of scientific questions'. Similarly, when they come to discuss mechanisms like the DMS–albedo link in more detail, they begin by reminding their readers that: 'while there would seem to be a very large number of possible bio-geochemical feedbacks, only a few have been identified and even these are not quantified'. But that is merely to tell students that there is research waiting to be done. The whole thrust of the book is that it is legitimate to think about such things, even if they are distantly inspired by an Earth goddess. Doubtless a generation trained using such books will do just that.

Gaia after Lovelock

> *The Gaia hypothesis was promoted to 'theory' status in the 1980s; however an explicit formal statement of it is not yet available ...*
>
> Lynn Margulis, 2000

So where *does* Gaia now stand? Well, the final verdict on the Gaia hypothesis – or hypotheses – is not yet in. And the outcomes from the discussion so far are interestingly mixed. The history of Gaia theory is certainly no simple story of a maverick scientist winning through, or of vindication of a scorned innovator. There is no question that the original intuition that there was something special about the Earth's environment which could best be accounted for by the evolution of the biosphere has been splendidly productive. As I have emphasised, it offers a nice case study in how a core idea which is partly metaphorical can itself evolve into a research programme. And invoking Gaia as shorthand for biosphere–geosphere interactions is no longer seen as a provocation by the upholders of scientific convention. As *Nature* opined soberly in the summer of 2000, 'James Lovelock's theory of the biotic regulation of Earth has now emerged with some respectability following close scrutiny by the biogeochemical community'. Whatever the under-lying reality that researchers are trying to uncover, there is a strong sense in which an idea is respect-able if enough of the right people say it is. In that sense, Gaia is more respectable now than ever.

But that does not mean that there is a large group of Gaian theorists espousing planetary homeostasis, still less optimisation of the Earth by life, for life. A generation after Gaia first appeared, new doubts continue to emerge as understanding of the past and present Earth continues to improve. And the variants of Gaia which are supported are almost invariably the less radical ones. The scientific communities involved have dealt with Gaia by assimilation, not conversion.

You can gauge this from the range of opinion represented at the second Chapman Conference of the American Geophysical Union devoted to Gaia, held in Valencia, Spain, in the middle of the year 2000. This was a slightly smaller affair than the first such meeting, though it heard more papers. From the abstracts, a larger proportion of the presentations this time around were focused on key aspects of Gaia, but the status of the grand hypothesis remained ambiguous. Lynn Margulis' note of her closing address, titled with characteristic boldness 'Modes of Confirmation of the Gaia Hypothesis', conceded that in spite of Gaia being elevated to a theory, it was still impossible to say exactly what it consisted of. She also insisted, though, that: 'The Gaia hypothesis of planetary modulation is implied if the term "Earth System Science" is used by the scientific community even when the "G-word" is avoided.'

However, other early enthusiasts for Gaia theory had modified their positions in interesting ways. Tyler Volk of New York University suggested that both planetary homeostasis and Daisyworld had outlived their usefulness as aids to understanding Gaia. *Contra* Margulis, he was concerned that Gaia would just reduce to a catchy name for Earth system science, which covers 'ten million lines of inquiry'. For the G-word to really mean something more, there must be large-scale principles which are generally applicable and connect all life and the environment. It is not yet clear exactly what these are, but Volk described his own efforts to derive measures of biological productivity which do not contain hidden assumptions about what counts as an environmental benefit.

A more unexpected pulling back from strong Gaia came from Lovelock's long-time friend and co-worker, and former PhD student, Andrew Watson, now a professor at the University of East Anglia in the UK. Watson, co-author of the first Daisyworld paper, is still deep in Earth system research, but is sceptical about the strong Gaian notion that the biosphere has emergent properties which more or less guarantee maintenance of environmental stability through homeostatic regulation.

Yes, there are Gaian biogeochemical mechanisms which stabilise the environment, says Watson. But there also appear to be others which can act as equally potent destabilisers. It could easily be that life on Earth has avoided disaster from positive feedbacks purely by chance. He is impressed, as others have been, by recent discoveries about Earth's distant climatic past which indicate that there have been very rapid changes, mainly leading to catastrophic cooling. In fact, there is growing evidence that the positive feedback from falling carbon dioxide levels in the atmosphere, glaciation, and ice reflecting sunlight back into space once led to such a temperature drop that the whole surface froze over, creating a 'snowball Earth'. The best evidence for this possibility dates from the pre-Cambrian, more than 2,000 million years ago, but some paleoclimatologists' readings of traces from past glaciations suggest that it may even have happened more than once.

So much for stability. Worse for Gaia, this was not something that life's supposed regulatory machinery could correct. The most likely explanation for the ultimate thaw, in fact, is a geochemical one. The ice cover would have reduced carbon dioxide absorption from weathering of silicate rocks, and eventually triggered greenhouse warming. The only other possibility seems to be volcanic activity. So it was old-fashioned non-biotic processes which provided the final climatic safety net.

What is more, the original snowballing could have been accelerated by the advent of land plants enhancing carbon dioxide absorption through different weathering processes, although there is no particular evidence that this took place. There *is* evidence, however, for positive biotic feedbacks accelerating the advent of later ice ages, which were basically triggered by reductions in solar radiation. What data there is seems to show that production of carbon dioxide and of methane, another green-house gas, increased during warming periods and decreased when the Earth's surface was cooling. Both would add to the change, not correct it.

Whatever happens on Daisyworld, on the real Earth Watson concludes that the biosphere is pretty bad at temperature regulation. 'We would have to conclude that Earth's system was not installed by a competent heating engineer', he writes, 'and there is no overriding principle that ensures that it works'. It is more like a botched DIY job, which is occasionally repaired after spectacular failures.

One world or many?

So there is new empirical data about ancient climates here which alters some of the arguments, and leaves Gaia looking distinctly ramshackle. It is also alarming for anyone tempted to take comfort from the idea that Gaia somehow maintains stability in the face of concerns about present-day global change. If the Earth system provides for positive – that is, destabilising – feedbacks as well as negative ones, then the consequences of human-induced carbon dioxide increase, for example, become more unpredictable. But this commentary also takes the discussion away from the details of global systems, which are now piling up with impressive speed, and back to more philosophical questions about Gaia, and about the limitations of all of the research which has been done to date.

The issue, as Watson points out, is chance versus necessity. Is a planet whose initial conditions are fit for life bound to evolve in ways which lead to global self-regulation? This is the implication which seems to follow for those who see Gaia as a giant example of a self-organising system, exemplifying important principles which are at work throughout the Universe. Or is the maintenance of the biosphere, even if it displays some of the features of Gaia, just down to dumb luck? On this view, like the apparently impressive cosmological fact that the constants of nature are fine-tuned in ways which allow stars and planets with complex chemistry to form, the fact that Earth systems do all the wonderful things they do has no special significance. It is simply a logical requirement of the fact that we are here to observe them. We are here because we are here.

This difference in views is never going to be resolved by the research programme whose growth I have tried to indicate. That is because Earth system science, however perfectly it comes to understand our own planet, is still after all confined to the Earth. And a single example of anything cannot be of any real help in deciding whether it came about by chance. However, there is a tantalising possibility here which did not exist when Gaian thought first began. In the last decade, early hints that astronomical observations could reveal planets orbiting nearby stars in our galaxy have grown into a rapidly expanding catalogue of new worlds. A claimed twenty-five planets were found in a single week in June 2002. With current techniques, the ones which are observable are large – the size of Jupiter or bigger. But there are plans afoot to search for smaller planets from orbiting satellites.

Both NASA and the European Space Agency (ESA) are on the way to launching missions which will use new instruments to survey large numbers of stars.

In the next ten to twenty years, NASA's Terrestrial Planet Finder (TPF) and ESA's projected Darwin mission should launch arrays of orbital telescopes flying in formation. They should be able to analyse infra-red spectra from planets whose size is similar to Earth, supposing there are any, and which are the right distance from their parent star to carry liquid water. The idea – which descends directly from Lovelock's original thinking about Mars – is that it ought to be possible to detect ozone, which can only derive from an atmosphere rich in oxygen. Visit one of these putative extra-solar worlds, in other words, and you would be able to strike a match. That, in turn, would signify the presence of life.

If this gets results, it will be pretty stunning news. But it will also shed new light on Gaia. If the astronomers can find enough planets out there which show chemical signs of life, it should then be possible to tell if there is more chance of finding planets with life around old or young stars. If they are more common around old stars, that could be because life takes a long time to appear. The history of the Earth suggests otherwise, however, so it could also mean that once life takes hold it has a good chance of maintaining conditions to its liking. On the other hand, if living planets mostly orbit young stars, that will suggest that life appears relatively often, but tends not to survive very long – so we are among the lucky ones. The third option is that none is found at all, which will indicate that either the appearance or the endurance of life, or perhaps both, are extremely rare. E.T. will be firmly consigned again to science fiction.

For now, this is all speculation and it is a matter of taste whether any one of these options would increase or reduce our wonder at the properties of our own Earth. It seems pretty wonderful to me whatever the astronomers find tied to some other star, and as it is the only habitable planet we have, its scientific as well as its sentimental interest will remain high, too. But this kind of more distant observation, which may well yield answers in the next few decades, does produce one pleasing result. Whatever their resonance in the contemporary debates over global change on Earth, Gaia theories' views of our home will develop, as they began, through the search for life on other planets.

FURTHER READING

Much of the story told here is pieced together from James Lovelock's own writings, especially his recent autobiography *Homage to Gaia*. The prefaces to the various editions of his earlier books, *Gaia* and *The Ages of Gaia*, which remain in print, also discuss the development of his ideas and his responses to critics. This 'horse's mouth' history is a fine thing to have, of course – it is his hypothesis, after all. But like anyone in the thick of a debate, Lovelock says different things at different times, and emphasises what suits his polemical purpose. The same is true of Lynn Margulis and her co-writer Dorion Sagan, whose occasional essays on Gaia are collected in *Slanted Truths: Essays on Gaia, Symbiosis and Evolution* (Copernicus Books, 1997). Among Margulis' other non-technical books, the best is also a co-production with Sagan, junior: *Microcosmos: Four Billion Years of Microbial Evolution* (Allen and Unwin, 1987).

The full set of papers from the first Chapman Conference, including James Kirchner's critique of the various Gaia hypotheses, is collected in *Scientists on Gaia*, edited by Stephen Schneider and Penelope Boston (MIT Press, 1991). The papers from the second Chapman Conference in 2000, including Andrew Watson's *Gaia and Observer Self-Selection*, are due to appear in book form as *Scientists on Gaia II*, edited by J. Miller and P. Boston (MIT Press), around the time this book is published, but you can read full abstracts at http:bioweb.uv.es/gaia2000/Libroact.pdf

For current research, the weekly journal *Nature* now, as in the past, seems more prone to publish papers and reviews relevant to Gaia than its American counterpart *Science*. One relatively recent example worth going into the archive for is Tim Lenton's 'Gaia and natural selection', *Nature*, 30 July 1998, vol. 394, pp. 439–47. The late Bill Hamilton's Gaian-inspired work with Lenton on oceanic microbes and cloud cover is clearly described in Lynn Hunt, 'Send in the Clouds', *New Scientist*, 30 May 1998, pp. 28–33. The latest episode in the iodine story is described in Charles E. Kolb, 'Iodine's air of importance', *Nature*, 6 June 2002, vol. 417, pp. 597–8.

For history, a fully annotated English translation of Vernadsky's *The Biosphere* finally appeared in

1998, with an introduction by Jacques Grinevald which puts this essay in the context of Vernadsky's career (Copernicus Books, 1998). Lawrence Joseph's *Gaia – the Growth of an Idea* (St Martin's Press, New York, 1990) is a useful and admirably balanced account of Gaia's development up to the end of the 1980s, and covers cults of the Earth goddess along with scientific developments. Scholarly attention to this whole revolutionary episode has so far been surprisingly slight, but Gaia is beginning to appear in the closing sections of histories of Earth sciences. The most useful treatment of this kind so far is in David Oldroyd, *Thinking about the Earth: A History of Ideas in Geology* (The Athlone Press, 1996).

For the interaction between eco-science and religion, the most interesting source is Connie Barlow's *Green Space, Green Time: The way of science* (Copernicus Books, 1999), an intriguing argument for incorporating Gaia into a new myth which underpins environmentally sound values.

The textbooks referred to in the closing chapter are:

Brian Skinner and Stephen C. Porter, *The Blue Planet – An Introduction to Earth System Science* (John Wiley, 1995).

Samuel Butcher, Robert Charlson, Gordon Orians and Gordon Wolfe (eds), *Global Biogeochemical Cycles* (Academic Press, International Geophysics Series), vol. 50, 1992.

Michael Jacobsen, Robert Charlson, Henning Rodhe and Gordon Orians (eds), *Earth System Science – From Biogeochemical Cycles to Global Change* (Academic Press, International Geophysics Series), vol. 72, 2000.

The last is a superb compendium of the details of processes which I have mostly drawn a veil over here by the (I hope) excusable abbreviation 'complex' – and a useful guide to the ones yet to be worked out.

For general geological and paleontological background, see Stephen Drury, *Stepping Stones: The making of our home world* (Oxford University Press, 1999). Drury is clear that life influences atmosphere and climate, but sees no evidence for Gaian homeostasis over the long haul. His wide-ranging and very readable synthesis brings home how powerful are the geological forces which life has to contend with.

If you want to know anything at all about NASA, future space missions, or extra-solar planets, or just want to sample images of the Earth, their website (www.nasa.gov) has a budget the size of a small country. The European Space Agency (ESA) details the other missions in prospect, slightly less lavishly (www.esa.int).

Other science titles available from
Icon Books:

Dawkins vs. Gould

Kim Sterelny

'Book of the Month' – *Focus* magazine

'Slim and readable ... the aficionado of evolutionary theory and the intense debate it engenders would do well to read it.' *Nature*

'A deft little book ... its insights are both useful and fun' *The Australian*

Science has seen its fair share of punch-ups over the years, but one debate, in the field of biology, has become notorious for its intensity. Over the last twenty years, Richard Dawkins and Stephen Jay Gould have engaged in a savage battle over evolution that shows no sign of waning.

Kim Sterelny moves beyond caricature to expose the *real* differences between the conceptions of evolution of these two leading scientists. He shows that the conflict extends beyond evolution to their very beliefs in science itself; and, in Gould's case, to domains in which science plays no role at all.

ISBN 1-84046-249-3   Paperback   £5.99

The Discovery of the Germ

John Waller

From Hippocrates to Louis Pasteur, the medical profession relied on almost wholly mistaken ideas as to the cause of infectious illness. Bleeding, induced vomiting and mysterious nostrums remained staple remedies. Surgeons, often wearing butcher's aprons caked in surgical detritus, blithely spread infection from patient to patient.

Then came the germ revolution: after two decades of scientific virtuosity, outstanding feats of intellectual courage and bitter personal rivalries, doctors at last realised that infectious diseases are caused by microscopic organisms.

Perhaps the greatest single advance in the history of medical thought, the discovery of the germ led directly to safe surgery, large-scale vaccination programmes, dramatic improvements in hygiene and sanitation, and the pasteurisation of dairy products. Above all, it set the stage for the brilliant emergence of antibiotic medicine to which so many of us now owe our lives.

In this book, John Waller provides a gripping insight into twenty years in the history of medicine that profoundly changed the way we view disease.

ISBN 1-84046-373-2   Hardback   £9.99

An Entertainment for Angels

Patricia Fara

'A concise, lively account.' Jenny Uglow, author of *The Lunar Men* (2002)

'Neat and stylish ... Fara's account of Benjamin Franklin's circle of friends and colleagues brings them squabbling, eureka-ing to life.' *The Guardian*

'Vividly captures the ferment created by the new science of the Enlightenment ... Fara deftly shows how new knowledge emerged from a rich mix of improved technology, medical quackery, Continental theorising, religious doubt and scientific rivalry.' *New Scientist*

'Combines telling anecdote with wise commentary ... presents us with numerous tasty and well-presented historical morsels.' *Times Higher Education Supplement*

Electricity was the scientific fashion of the Enlightenment, 'an Entertainment for Angels, rather than for Men'. Patricia Fara tells the engrossing tale of the strange birth of electrical science – from a high-society party trick to a symbol of man's emerging dominance over nature.

ISBN 1-84046-348-1   Hardback   £9.99

Eureka!

Andrew Gregory

'Marvel as Andrew Gregory explains how the Greeks destroyed myths and gods in favour of a rule-based cosmos ... A readable, pocket-sized primer and a worthwhile present for anyone who needs to fill in the gaps in their knowledge.' *New Scientist*

Eureka! shows that science began with the Greeks. Disciplines as diverse as medicine, biology, engineering, mathematics and cosmology all have their roots in ancient Greece. Plato, Aristotle, Pythagoras, Archimedes and Hippocrates were amongst its stars – master architects all of modern, as well as ancient, science. But what lay behind this colossal eruption of scientific activity?

Free from intellectual and religious dogma, the Greeks rejected explanation in terms of myths and capricious gods, and, in distinguishing between the natural and the supernatural, they were the first to discover nature. New theories began to be developed and tested, leading to a rapid increase in the sophistication of knowledge, and ultimately to an awareness of the distinction between science and technology.

Andrew Gregory unravels the genesis of science in this fascinating exploration of the origins of Western civilisation and our desire for a rational, legitimating system of the universe.

ISBN 1-84046-289-2   Hardback   £9.99

Knowledge is Power

John Henry

Francis Bacon, the renowned English statesman and man of letters, is a leading figure in the history of science. Yet he never made a major discovery, provided a lasting explanation of any physical phenomena or revealed any hidden laws of nature. How then can he rank alongside the likes of Isaac Newton – one of the finest scientists of them all?

Bacon was the first major thinker to describe how science should be done, and to explain why it should be done that way. Against the tide of his times, he rejected the gathering of scientific knowledge for its own sake. Instead, he saw the bounty of science in terms of practical benefit to mankind, and its advance as a means to improve the daily lives of his contemporaries. But foremost, and thus making by far his greatest contribution, Bacon promoted the use of experimentation, coming to outline and define the rigorous procedures of the 'scientific method' that today forms the very bedrock of modern scientific progress.

In this fascinating and accessible book, John Henry gives a dramatic account of the background to Bacon's innovations and the sometimes unconventional sources for his ideas. He explains how magic, civil service bureaucracy and the belief in a forthcoming apocalypse came together in the creation of Bacon's legacy, why he was so concerned to revolutionise the attitude to scientific knowledge – and why his ideas for reform still resonate today.

ISBN 1-84046-356-2   Hardback   £9.99

Latitude & the Magnetic Earth

Stephen Pumfrey

'A chunky read with much more to it than first meets the eye. [Stephen Pumfrey] marshals his scientific and philosophical themes impressively while adding flesh to the hitherto enigmatic Gilbert.' *New Scientist*

'This bijou volume is most valuable for its insights ... It is as much for his method as for his conclusions that we should remember this great Elizabethan.' *TLS*

William Gilbert (1544–1603) was royal physician to Queen Elizabeth I and the most distinguished man of science to emerge from her reign. He is the inventor of the term 'electricity', the father of electrical studies, the creator of modern magnetic science and – most famously – the discoverer of the Earth's magnetic nature. Yet, incredibly, he is largely unknown.

Gilbert's close contact with the elite mariners of Elizabethan London enabled him to learn of the magnetic compass and of the strange behaviour of its magnetised needle – a phenomenon known as the magnetic 'dip'. Using a pioneering experimental method, he came to realise that the Earth is a giant magnet; a great body imbued with a 'magnetic soul' that drove it forward in its Copernican orbit. In this golden age of circumnavigations of the globe and of the founding of new colonies, he was the first to use magnetism to determine the latitude of a ship at sea. Alongside these discoveries, Gilbert's writings – some even proposing to solve the problem of longitude – challenged the scientific orthodoxy of his day, and boldly led the battle to establish our modern ideas of terrestrial magnetism.

Lively and accessible, *Latitude & the Magnetic Earth* – the first new exploration of Gilbert for forty years – brings the story up to date, leaving the reader with a vivid feel not only for the conflicts surrounding Gilbert's discoveries and his scientific legacy, but for the man himself.

ISBN 1-84046-290-6   Hardback   £9.99

How Far is Up?

John & Mary Gribbin

How far is it to the edge of the Universe? Less than eighty years ago astronomers began to realise that the Milky Way galaxy in which we live is just one island in an immense ocean of space.

Award-winning authors John and Mary Gribbin tell the story of how the cosmic distance scale was measured, the personalities involved and the increasingly sophisticated instruments they used. Astronomers can now study light from objects so distant that it has taken ten billion years on its journey across space to us, travelling all the time at a speed of 300,000 kilometres per second: that's how far up is!

ISBN 1-84046-439-9   Hardback   £9.99

The Manhattan Project

Jeff Hughes

Established in 1942 at the height of the Second World War, the Manhattan Project was a dramatic quest to beat the Nazis to a deadly goal: the atomic bomb. At Los Alamos and several other sites, American, British, Canadian and refugee European scientists, together with engineers, technicians and many other workers, laboured to design and build nuclear weapons. Their efforts produced 'Little Boy' and 'Fat Man', the bombs that ultimately destroyed Hiroshima and Nagasaki in August 1945.

A vast and secret 'state within a state', the Manhattan Project cost $2 billion. It catapulted scientists – particularly nuclear scientists – to positions of intellectual prestige and political influence. State funds flowed for science as never before, and led to the creation of huge new research institutes, especially large particle accelerators designed to explore the properties of matter – like that at CERN, near Geneva. With their huge experiments, complex organisation and lavish funding, these institutes represented a new form of scientific organisation: 'Big Science'.

Yet, from the large astronomical telescopes of the nineteenth century to the factory-like laboratories of the 1930s, 'Big Science' has a social and scientific history that long pre-dates the advent of the atom bomb. Arguing that the Manhattan Project both drew on and accelerated a trend already well under way, Jeff Hughes offers a lively reinterpretation of the key elements in the history and mythology of twentieth-century science.

ISBN 1-84046-376-7   Hardback   £9.99

Perfect Copy

Nicholas Agar

Cloning represents some of the most exciting – and some of the most morally complex – science of our time.

In 1997 Ian Wilmut and his team announced that they had done the impossible: they had cloned a mammal from an adult cell. This breakthrough prompted immediate calls for the new technology to be used on humans. Italian fertility specialist Severino Antinori hopes to use cloning to give infertile couples the opportunity to at last become parents. Cloning may also solve, once and for all, the problem of rejection that bedevils transplant surgery. Perhaps it even holds the secret of eternal life.

But plans to clone humans have triggered an international storm of protest. Scientists, including Wilmut, politicians from left and right, and theologians from almost all religions find the idea not just unsavoury, but abhorrent.

In this book, Nicholas Agar provides a uniquely accessible exploration of this highly controversial issue. Starting with the biology, and building up the scientific background step by step, *Perfect Copy* provides the perfect guide to the moral labyrinth that surrounds the cloning debate.

ISBN 1-84046-380-5   Paperback   £7.99

Watt's Perfect Engine

Ben Marsden

James Watt is synonymous with the steam engine, that Promethean symbol of the Industrial Revolution. But what motivated Watt to re-invent steam? What convinced him that the stunningly simple idea of giving Thomas Newcomen's ubiquitous fire-engine a 'separate condenser' could work in practice, banish waste – and achieve perfection? And how did Watt's perfect engine become the progenitor of progress, and its problems, in nineteenth-century Britain?

The astonishing success of steam meant taking a tiny classroom toy and thinking big, re-equipping industry with a new factory power. That meant cashing in on connections and re-deploying instrument makers' skills. It meant conspiring with enlightened philosophers, like chemist Joseph Black, ensconced in Glasgow's ancient College, and the hard-nosed entrepreneurs, like buckle-maker Matthew Boulton, who consorted for the sake of commerce at Birmingham's Lunar Society.

This is a tale of science and technology in tandem, of factory show-spaces and international espionage, of bankruptcy and braindrains, lobbying and legislation, and patents and pirates. It is a story of boiling kettles and leaking cylinders, mechanisms perfected, monopolies defended, and competitors trounced. And this is a book about another kind of perfection: taking the man James Watt, warts and all, and making an icon fit for an age of invention.

ISBN 1-84046-361-9   Hardback   £9.99